TOMBSTONE:
A CHRONICLE IN PERSPECTIVE

By Gary Ledoux

Produced by:

Clum & Company Old-West Productions
PO Box 466
Moreno Valley, CA 92556
e-mail: clumandcompany@aol.com

CLUM & CO.

OLD-WEST PRODUCTIONS

First Edition: October 2002

National Library of Canada Cataloguing in Publication

Ledoux, Gary
        Tombstone : a chronicle in perspective / Gary Ledoux.

ISBN 1-55395-129-8

        I. Title.

F819.T6L42 2002   979.1'53   C2002-904520-7

PRINTED IN CANADA

This book was published *on-demand* in cooperation with Trafford Publishing.
On-demand publishing is a unique process and service of making a book available for retail sale to the public taking advantage of on-demand manufacturing and Internet marketing.
On-demand publishing includes promotions, retail sales, manufacturing, order fulfilment, accounting and collecting royalties on behalf of the author.

Suite 6E, 2333 Government St., Victoria, B.C. V8T 4P4, CANADA
Phone   250-383-6864   Toll-free   1-888-232-4444 (Canada & US)
Fax   250-383-6804   E-mail   sales@trafford.com
Web site   www.trafford.com   TRAFFORD PUBLISHING IS A DIVISION OF TRAFFORD HOLDINGS LTD.
Trafford Catalogue #02-0843   www.trafford.com/robots/02-0843.html

10   9   8   7   6   5   4   3   2

Table Of Contents

Foreword

What Is Time? 4
The Old West Defined 5
Time Has Been Kind 6
A World-Wide Phenomenon 7
Why The Fascination With The Old West? 8
Why The Fascination With Wyatt Earp? 9
Why The Fascination With Tombstone? 9
Not Another Earp Book! 10

The Chronicle

1600 – 2002   402 Years of Tombstone History 11

The Perspective

Clips, Quips and Musings On History 116
Time Travel 119
Boom-Town "Baby-Boomers" 120
When Did The Old West End? 123
Photo Gallery 125

Appendix

Have Bar Will Travel 133
John P. Clum – A Life 135
How Could He Go Wrong? 147
Who Is Buried In Morgan Earp's Grave? 148
Hamburgers and Gunslingers 150
Frederick Jackson Turner: The Unappreciated Orator 154
The Significance Of The Frontier In American History 155
About Clum & Co. 170
Gun Safety Message 171
Bibliography

Dedication

This book is dedicated to my wife, Rachel, for her patience during the many long hours it took to research, write, and produce this book. Thanks also for her help in getting the book printed.

This book is also dedicated to all the re-enactors, actors, craftspeople, and others that help keep alive the spirit and the knowledge of a by-gone era, the Old West.

Grateful Acknowledgement

Thanks also to author Earl Chaffin for his support, friendship and the sharing of his knowledge.

And a grateful acknowledgment goes to Kevin Smith of Moreno Valley, California for the cover art.

A special thanks also goes to the great folks at the Colton Public Library, Colton, California for their assistance in allowing access to their library's "Earp Files".

On the cover: The Tombstone Epitaph office and the Bird Cage Theatre, two of Tombstone's most enduring landmarks are coupled with Wyatt Earp (top) and John Clum (bottom), two of Tombstone's most endearing characters.

Disclaimer

The information contained herein is as accurate as humanly possible. Various research sources give conflicting dates for the same event or incident so some discrepancies may be present.

However, it is not the intent of this book to be a definitive guide to the exact dates for events and people surrounding Tombstone and the Old West. But rather it is a comparative study to accentuate the relativity of dates for events surrounding Tombstone and it's citizens, other "Old West" events, and other national and world events.

Forward

What Is Time?

We can measure time with a clock as the seconds, minutes, and hours pass by. We can measure it with a calendar as the days turn into weeks, weeks into months, and months into years. We can measure time by periods, ancient, medieval, and renaissance, and reformation. Time can be measured in terms of ages; the ice age, machine age, space age and information age.

But these are all man-made conventions contrived to lend a degree of practicality to deal with what is really an abstract yet profound intellectual concept. Time.

Time, in its abstract form might be described as continual flow of events that never stands still. Think what happens when you ask a person the time. By the time they hear your question, look at their watch, tell you the time, and your ears hear their voice and your brain processes the information, time has passed by and it is no longer THAT time!

Time passes, unceasingly, unrelenting in its forward march. It is only people, events, and circumstances that, within a framework of the human conventions of watches and calendars, that mark those places along its path.

Some might say the events are pre-destined while others subscribe to the belief that events happen randomly. In either case – they happen constantly.

While time itself is abstract, it is good that we ascribe a measurement to it thus enabling us to pinpoint precise pieces of time, and look back to see how all the events that happened during that period, be it a year, a day, or even a particular minute tie people and events together.

It is amazing also how one particular moment in time can have such a far-reaching effect influencing other parts of the world or influencing an entire culture for hundreds of years afterward. Consider the moment in time when the first shot was fired on Fort Sumter signaling the start of the Civil War. Or, to get a better feel for the concept, and to relate to events that many people alive today remember and how it changes their lives; consider the moment in time when President John F. Kennedy was shot. Or the moment Neil Armstrong set foot on the moon; or the moment when the World Trade Center collapsed.

In that vein, consider that moment on the afternoon of October 26, 1881 when eight men faced each other in a vacant lot behind a livery stable. Three men were "hurled into eternity in the duration of a moment" and Wyatt Earp and his brothers, totally unbeknownst to them at the time, became principals in what has become a world-wide phenomena – a period of time we call, the Old West!

We tend to think of the Old West as a singular spot in time – a freeze-frame in our history marked by gun battles, bawdy saloons, dusty streets and the sound of hoof beats. Well, it's all that, but it was then, as the time we live in now, a very fluid series of events. As the world changes around us every day (think of that 3 year old computer sitting on your desk and how "yester-teck" it is today) give some thought to what happened in Wyatt Earp's lifetime. Granted things did not move as fast then as they do now (or so it would seem), but change they did.

A defining moment in time came for me in December, 1993 when the credits rolled across a movie screen in a darkened theatre as Val Kilmer, Kurt Russell, Bill Paxton, and Sam Elliot marched down "Fremont Street" marking the end of the movie "Tombstone". I was already history buff in general and an Old West buff in particular. But that movie made me rabid for the Old West and the Tombstone phenomenon.

The Old West Defined

Inasmuch as the Old West can be defined by a time-period, most would agree that the Old West existed between the end of the Civil War, about 1865, and the turn of the 20th century in 1900. Some would place it at an earlier starting point; 1848 with the discovery of gold at Sutter's Mill and the start of the California gold rush.

The Old West can be further defined by a point of view of those who lived it. Each person, each diverse group of people, has a story to tell.

The story of the Old West can be told as an unbroken series of triumphs…and failures.

There are the stories of those who farmed the land. Farmed it until, through poor land management, literally wore-out the soil, and then moved on to greener pastures and more fertile soil.

Southerners that lost everything in the Civil War, their homes, their families, and their way of life relate countless stories. Many became successful in a new land with new opportunities.

There's the story told by the Irish leaving hard times and the squalid conditions of the crowded New York tenements to start a new life in wide-open spaces.

There's the story of the cowboy driving a herd of cattle to market. The pay was never much, but the lifestyle could not be matched anywhere else. They were free, had few material wants and needs, and could be as anonymous as they cared to be.

There's the story of those who worked the mines dragging ton after ton of gold and silver ore from the ground. It was hard work, dirty work, back-breaking work; but the pay was steady. And if a man was frugal, and watched his pennies, he could make a decent living – perhaps more so than opportunities offered elsewhere.

There were those who mined the land and drove the cattle and tilled the earth. And then there were those who mined the miners and drove the cow-boys, and tilled the farmers for their money. The saloon owners and soiled doves were some of the richest people in town.

Of course, there were those whose tales of success that went beyond the boundaries of imagination. The cattle barons, land barons, railroad magnates and mining speculators fueled the culture and economy of the new land.

Of course, things were not always rosy. Driven by desperation, hatred, vengeance, greed, or simply because they thought they could get away with it, the Old West was full of robbers, thieves, opportunists, con-men, killers, bank robbers, stage robbers, and other purveyors of violence and mayhem. For some, their story is quite short. Being on the wrong side of law tends to catch up with some people quite early in life.

There were the families that left a known way of life for the Unexpected but never came to know whatever that Unexpected was. Traveling in wagon trains they died on the trail from various diseases, complications of childbirth, accidents, Indian attacks, attacks by other settlers, death by drowning or heat stroke, or simply being lost on the trail and perishing to the elements.

The Chinese immigrants working long hard hours building America's railroads or working menial tasks for little pay tell yet a different story. Standing in stark contrast in culture, dress, and mannerisms to what we have come to know as the traditional "westerner", the Chinese helped build America, all the while suffering discrimination and other indignities at the hands of those for whom their labor benefited.

Of course, the story of the Old West cannot be told without including the plight of the Native Americans and Manifest Destiny. From the time the first Europeans landed on the eastern shores, each step westward became a step backward for Native Americans in a dizzying morass of failed policies, treaties and cultural experimentation. Today, Americans consider it unthinkable to be assaulted on our native soil. Consider the outcry spawned by the attacks on the World Trade Center on September 11, 2001 and the massive retaliation in Afghanistan. Then, step back 150 years. The massive herds of buffalo that gave the plains Indians their way of life, and were wiped out by encroaching civilization, was their World Trade Center.

The story of the West is one of expansionism, but at a great price. Had things been different, had another set of circumstances occurred, a different set of events transpired, America's western boundary could still stop at the Mississippi and Mexico could be our western, rather than southern neighbor. One could argue ad-infinitum the morality of the events between 1848 and 1900 that lead to the US becoming a continental nation. But it would be only that, an argument, and just so many words. Today, we can only look back at those events, learn from the past, and help define a better future.

There were law-men and law-breakers, bank presidents and bank robbers, stage drivers and stage robbers, settlers and squatters, actors and drummers, soiled doves and Chinese laundrymen, hard drinkers and tea sippers – all contributed to the fabric we call the Old West!

Time Has Been Kind

Time has been kind to the Old West. All the suffering and success, triumph and tragedy, life and death of that time has been softened by time and by so many writers and story-tellers. The Old West has been so romanticized in many movies, books, and magazine articles. Fact and fiction, myth and legend have been molded into a culture that is truly American but recognized the world over.

As a re-enactor, I get to "live" the Old West on many weekends and see the faces of audience members that love to see live action and hear the gunshots reminiscent of a time gone by. Despite what some may read in today's newspapers about an out crying of those who would totally ban firearms from private citizens, at least those that attend today's re-enactments seem to thoroughly enjoy themselves. Many people will approach the re-enactors after a show asking about the guns, the hats, the spurs, the ladies' fancy dresses – and ask if Tombstone was a real place or just some fictional town dreamed up for the movies!

6

To starkly illustrate how kind time has really been to the Old West, I will refer to a passage in Bob Boze Bell's book, "Bad Men, Outlaws, and Gunfighters Of The Old West" in which he describes a modern day train robbery in Mexico. On November 9, 1998 about a dozen bandits robbed the Chihuahua-Pacific Railroad as the train entered a tunnel. They hold-up the train for about 40 minutes, walking through the passenger cars waving their guns around and pistol-whipping some. Perhaps thinking that the whole thing was a put-on, a tourist tries to video-tape the robbery and is shot dead. Several others were wounded and all were terrorized. The bandits leapt off the train and disappeared into the thick underbrush. Nobody cheered, nobody applauded, many wept.

In contrast, in August, 2001, my wife and I joined up with a number of re-enactors in Virginia City and arranged an "Old West train robbery re-enactment" of the Virginia-Truckee railroad which carries tourists from Virginia City to a neighboring town, a distance of about 7 miles. As the train pulled into the station, "bandits" came out of hiding, called for all passengers to "throw up your hands" and demanded money and valuables. "Fortunately", some "law-men" happened to riding the train that day. Stepping off the train the "law-men" faced-down the bandits, a raucous gunfight ensued and the bad-men were "ultimately dispatched with fervor". One small child, scared by the noise, cried. Everyone else cheered and applauded.

Perhaps some day, as Bob Boze Bell puts it, maybe in the year 2098, that train robbery of November 9, 1998 will be re-enacted and people will applaud and cheer.

A World-Wide Phenomenon

As a re-enactor and Old West enthusiast my wife, Rachel, and I individually, and with re-enactor groups have traveled to places like Tombstone and Holbrook, Arizona, Virginia City, Nevada, and Calico and Julian, California.

Dressed in our full Old West regalia we sometimes perform and sometimes, even if we are not performing, by default because of the way we are dressed, get to interact and talk with many tourists. It is enlightening, and makes me proud to not only be an American, but to be a part of the Old West re-enactment community, to talk to the many people that come from other countries to see, specifically, places like Tombstone or Calico. These are places they have only read about or seen in movies and are now visiting to "soak-up" some of that Old West culture. Those tourists from other countries can be fascinating to talk to. They love to talk about the Old West, many asking how true the movie "Tombstone" really was. That is - if they speak English! For those that don't, they will usually point to their camera and ask in broken English to have their picture taken with "The Sheriff". Rachel and I sometimes laugh about how our picture is in so many family albums all over the world!

While traveling in Central and South America on business, I turned on the television in my hotel room only to see a John Wayne western playing – with dubbed-in Spanish. (Seeing the Duke habla espanol takes some getting used-to)

While attending the Single Action Shooting Society's "End Of Trail" in Norco, California, one of the largest and most popular "Old West style" live-shooting events in the world, I happened across a gentleman working as a waddie. (event helper) Despite being from Holland, he was dressed out quite smartly for the event in his Old West period clothes, pocket watch and Stetson. He looked good in every respect – except for his wooden shoes!

You see, he lived in the Netherlands and was able to get everything he needed via the internet, everything except his boots which he planned to buy from a suttler at End Of Trail. He had traveled all the way across the Atlantic to attend a real Old West event in the American west. He noted that there were many re-enactors and Old West enthusiasts in his home country but that it was hard to get into the culture against a back-drop of windmills and tulips!

And of course, there is ubiquitous internet. It is astounding to web-surf across all the various Old West web sites with their links to other sites, and see how many re-enactor groups there are all over Europe. At first glance it seems unlikely to watch a re-enactment of the OK Corral gunfight against the backdrop of a medieval English castle. But, of course, those that settled the west from 1848 to 1900 had to come from somewhere and many came from European countries.

Bless them all, in Europe, The Netherlands, and Central and South America for keeping alive the stories, the legends and the myths of the Old West.

Why The Fascination With The Old West?

It was a time when men, women, and families could start over again in a new land where opportunities were boundless. Some moved west escaping the ravages of the Civil War, some the squalor of big-city living on the east coast. Some looked for riches, some looked for anonymity, some for a new identity. In a time before computers and mountains of demographic information, a man (or woman) could travel from town to town and be a different person in each town – a new identity.

The Old West is well documented. Despite many people having a relatively low education rate, many people kept diaries and thus we have some of the most poignant documentation of life in the Old West. It is fascinating today to read the story of a family traveling west via wagon train, or hear about the day-to-day events in Tombstone from George W. Parsons or the events of Contention City from George Hand. Ironically, people like Wm F. Cody and Frederick Remington realized they were living in a time that would soon vanish forever and thus from Cody was born the first Old West re-enactments and Remington gave us visual images that will last forever.

Although the people living during that time may not have thought so, today we think of the Old West as a slower-paced time – something we may long-for today! There were no telephones (at least early-on), no televisions, no computers and no internet. People were not subjected to a constant barrage of advertising from radios, billboards, and TV. A commute to work meant a short walk across town or a short ride of a few miles from your ranch into town. People got together at church socials or minstrel shows or at the local saloon. There was no e-mail!

It seems no matter what period of history you can think of; time has a way of softening and romanticizing that era, even in our own lifetime. Today when we think of the 1950's, we conjure up visions of hot rods, slicked-back DA pompadour hairstyles on the boys and poodle skirts on the girls and everything was rosy under President Eisenhower. Yet, the threat of utter nuclear annihilation at the hands of the "Red Menace" was very real and always hovering at the outer edge of our consciousness while we enjoyed our burgers and fries and the drive-in.

Why The Fascination With Wyatt Earp?

First, contrary to many fictional western movies and TV shows, rarely did the good guy face-down the bad guy out in the dusty street. Mostly, they ambushed each other, jumping from behind a tree or bushes or sneaking up behind their foe. To wit; Wild Bill Hickok was shot from behind by Jack McCall, Jesse James, while adjusting a picture on the wall was shot from behind by Bob Ford, Morgan Earp's enemies shot him in the back as he played pool, and Billy The Kid was ambushed in a dark room by Sheriff Pat Garrett.

In the case on the OK Corral shootout, eight men faced each other in an open vacant lot and despite lead flying everywhere; Wyatt Earp was the only one to walk away without a scratch thus giving him almost a mystical aura. You might say he was the "Superman" of his time.

Second, the OK Corral shootout was not only one of those rare occasions where men faced each other squarely in the street. It is arguably one of the best-documented events of its type ever. With the *Nugget* and *Epitaph* each pouring gallons of ink on paper about the subject, and all the subsequent books and articles about not only the event, but also the time prior to and after the event, it is a veritable "Super Bowl" of the Old West making all who were associated with it, famous.

Perhaps Wyatt Earp fascinates us because of the time he lived in. In a time when the average life expectancy was relatively low, and perhaps even lower if you were part of the crowd that Wyatt ran with, Wyatt lived all through the Old West period and well into the 20th century. Although the Old West seems like a time and place of so long ago, it is interesting to think that there are people alive today (2002) who *could* have known Wyatt Earp.

Finally, while described as being dour or laconic by contemporaries, (as opposed to his purported jolly brother, Virgil) Wyatt Earp has emerged through the mist of time as a most charismatic character with many thanks to Kurt Russell, Kevin Costner, Hugh O' Brian and many others who have portrayed the "Lion Of Tombstone". The myths, the legends, the truth and everything in-between all add up to a captivating yet enigmatic man.

Why The Fascination With Tombstone?

Dodge City, Leadville, Calico, Bodie, are all great-sounding names for an Old West town. All conjure up scenes of buckskin-clad men with six-guns, woman with large bonnets and dusty streets. But let's face it – nothing says Old West like a town with a name like Tombstone. The very inference of its name says gun-fight and a boot-hill full of men who were just a little bit slow on the trigger. Chances are, there will never be another town named Tombstone. Think how politically incorrect that would be today!

The other great thing about Tombstone, and why it continues to capture our imagination, is that, unlike many Old West towns that grew up, changed, and saw urban renewal, one can still visit many of the same places today that were frequented by the Tombstoners of 1881. All the streets are still laid out as they were in 1881.

Although the Bird Cage Theatre has seen some changes, (during the 1930's it was a coffee shop) it remains pretty much as it was when Curley Bill and Johnny Ringo enjoyed a show there.

One can stand at the bar today at the Crystal Palace just like Wyatt and Virgil did so many years before. Or have a meal at Nellie Cashman's restaurant, formerly the Russ House owned by Nellie Cashman, which has been in the same place for over 120 years.

The Grand Hotel, as a hotel, is gone now. But the building still remains and you can visit what was then the lobby and have a beer at Big Nose Kate's Saloon, one of Tombstone's favorite "watering holes".

And of course, the coup-de gras of a trip to Tombstone, the OK Corral is still there and one can see how the gunfight happened 121 years ago, several times a day.

Not Just Another Earp Book!

This is not just another book about the Earps and Tombstone! It is not yet another retelling of the same (albeit fascinating) stories of the early 1880's in southeastern Arizona. In fact, this book doesn't really tell a story at all!

On the contrary, it makes one think (I hope) about how all the stories you've ever ready about Tombstone and the Earps and the Clantons and McLaury's interrelate in the context of time and associations with other people and places and events.

When we read books about the Old West, they tend to focus on a particular person, event or concept. They might deal solely with Billy The Kid or Butch and Sundance. They might deal with a single event like the Oklahoma Land Rush or the massacre at Wounded Knee. They might deal solely with concepts like cattle drives or building the railroads.

When I first started reading about the settling of the west, I began to wonder how it all fit together and who or what came first. Each book or article I read about the Old West was fascinating in and of itself but, until I started this book and building this time-line, I never really grasped the concept of how it all fit together.

Using the "Tombstone Time-Line Concept", showing other Old West, world, national and pop-culture events alongside Tombstone-related events helped define for me, the Old West, and how it all fit together.

The Chronicle – 402 Years Of Tombstone History

Date	Tombstone Events	Other Old West Events	Events Elsewhere
1600, Circa	The first recorded Earp, John Earp is born in Staffordshire, England marking the first generation of Earps. Little does he realize that with his birth, a dynasty is formed that will last into the 21st century.		Shakespeare writes *Hamlet*.
1607, May 13			Jamestown, Virginia is established.
1631, Circa	Thomas Earp, son of John Earp is born in Ireland marking the second generation of Earps.		Boston has its first serious fire causing wooden chimneys and thatched roofs to be banned.
1632, June 20			A charter for the settlement of Maryland is granted to Cecilius Calvert.
1656	Thomas Earp Jr. is born marking the third generation of Earps.		A Captain Kemble of Boston is forced to sit in the stocks for two hours for the crime of lewdly kissing his wife on Sunday. He had just returned from a three year sea voyage.
1670, Circa	Thomas Earp Jr. is the first Earp to arrive in America in present day Maryland.		US population is estimated at 114,500.
1674, December 4			The first permanent building in what is now Chicago is established. It is a mission built by Father Jacques Marquette.
1769, July 16		Mission San Diego de Alcala, the first of twenty-one, is established in California.	
1770		Mission San Carlos is established in Carmel Valley, California.	
1771		Mission San Antonio de Padua and Mission San Gabriel Arcangel are established in California.	
1772		Mission San Luis Obispo de Tolosa is established.	
1776		Mission San Francisco de Asis and Mission San Juan Capistrano is established.	The Declaration of Independence is signed in Philadelphia.
1777		Mission Santa Clara de Asis is established.	
1782		Mission San Buenaventura is established. Know as the "place of canales" the padres teach the Indians how to dam-up water and irrigate crops.	
1786		Mission Santa Barbara is established.	

11

Date	Tombstone Events	Other Old West Events	Events Elsewhere
1787	Walter Earp, father to Nicholas Porter Earp and grandfather to Wyatt Earp is born in Maryland.	Mission La Purisma Concepcion is established.	The Northwest Ordinance enacted by Congress establishes the Northwest Territory of the United States.
1790	Martha Ann Early is born. She will marry Walter Earp in 1808 and she and Walter will become Wyatt Earp's grandmother and grandfather.		Congress authorizes the first US Census. At that time, 3,929,625 live in the US – the biggest city is Philadelphia.
1791		Mission Santa Cruz and Mission Nuestra Senora de la Soledad is established.	
1797		Mission San Jose, Mission San Juan Bautista, San Miguel de Arcangel and San Fernando Rey de Espana are established.	
1798		Mission San Luis rey de Francia is established.	
1804, May 14		Mission Santa Ines is established.	The Lewis and Clark expedition to explore the northwest and Oregon Territory leaves St. Louis MO.
1806, September 23			The Lewis and Clark expedition return to St. Louis effectively opening up The West.
1813, September 6	Nicholas Porter Earp, father to Wyatt Earp, is born.		
1814, July 19		Future gun-maker Samuel Colt is born.	
1817		Mission San Raffael Arcangle is established.	
1823		Mission San Francisco de Solano is established.	
1825, Summer		The first mountain-man rendezvous is held at Henry's Fork near present-day Burntfork, Wyoming. Here, over the course of several weeks, the mountain men will sell the furs they have been trapping all winter and secure provisions for another year in the mountains. This event will go on until 1840 when the demand for fur will have dwindled, and encroaching western migration will end this era in American history.	With the start of the Nashua (NH) Manufacturing Company in 1823 (and other similar enterprises along New England waterways) the industrial age is in full swing.
1826		The Abbott-Downing Company is formed in Concord, NH to build what would be more popularly known as the Concord Stagecoach. The company would last under various name changes until 1899 building over 3000 Concords Stagecoaches. The Stagecoach would be used in remote corners of the West well into the 20th century.	

Date	Tombstone Events	Other Old West Events	Events Elsewhere
1830, June 12	Pima County Sheriff, and Wells-Fargo Agent Bob Paul is born in Lowell, MA. He will later be friends with the Earps in Tombstone.		
1830, August 28			The first locomotive built in America, the "Tom Thumb" debuts in Baltimore.
1832, January 14			The first street car pulled by horses debuts in New York City.
1833	*The Arizona Citizen* Over his long career, famed Tombstone mayor, John P. Clum was associated with several newspapers, the most prominent of course being the *Tombstone Epitaph*. He was however the proprietor of *The Arizona Citizen* of Tucson, Arizona from November 1877 to February 1880 when he sold it. The following pages carry several excerpts from *The Arizona Citizen* dated Saturday, November 29, 1879.	Future well-known thespian, Edwin Booth is born. As well known as he will be in his time, his brother, John Wilkes Booth will become even more famous, or infamous, when he assassinates President Lincoln. The Mexican Congress passes the Act Of Secularization effectively obliterating the Missions system in California.	
1835, November 30			Samuel Clemens aka Mark Twain is born.
1836 February 25		Samuel Colt receives a patent for his first revolver, the Colt .45.	The siege of the Alamo by Mexican President Santa Anna is in it's second day. 187 Texans will hold off the assault until March 6.
1836, September 1		A wagon train of missionaries, led by Dr. Marcus Whitman arrives in Walla Walla at the Columbia and Snake Rivers. This is one of the earliest wagon trains to make the trek west with a group of women.	
1837, May 27		James Butler Hickok, better known as Wild Bill Hickok is born in Homer, Illinois.	Economic problems in the US lead to a financial panic. Banks begin to fail leading to widespread unemployment.
1837, October 7	Newton Jasper Earp, half brother to Wyatt, is born. At the time, father Nicholas Porter Earp is married to his first wife, Abigail Storm.		Beginning with the production of sturdy, steel plows, the John Deere Company of Vermont begins to grow.
1839, January 24	Sister to Newton Jasper, Mariah Ann Earp is born. She will live only a month.		
1839, February 13	Sister to Newton Jasper, Mariah Ann Earp dies.		
1839, February 20			Dueling, a commonly accepted way of settling disputes, is outlawed in the District Of Columbia.
1839, October 8	Abigail Storm, wife to Nicholas Porter Earp dies at age 26.		

Date	Tombstone Events	Other Old West Events	Events Elsewhere
1840, July 30	Nicholas Porter Earp marries Virginia Ann Cooksey. She will become the mother to the famous Earp brothers.		During 1840, The Washingtonian Temperance Society is founded in Baltimore. Despite their efforts, imbibing will continue to be a major past-time, especially for men, until prohibition some 80 years later.
1840, Summer		The last mountain man rendezvous is held at the Green River at the confluence of Horse Creek near present-day Pinedale, Wyoming. Although some will continue to trap and hunt beyond this point, an encroaching western population and the fact that many animals have been trapped and shot almost to extinction pretty much ends this way of life.	
1841, June 28	James Cooksey Earp is born in Hartford, KY.		
1841, Other Events		Leslie Fort Blackburn is born in New York. He will later become a Deputy US Territorial Marshal for the Arizona Territory with an office at 216 Fifth Street in Tombstone.	
1843, July 11	Virgil Walter Earp born in Hartford KY.		Oregon settlers establish a provisional government at Champoeg.
1843, August 26			The typewriter is patented.
1844, December			Nitrous oxide, laughing gas, is used for the first time as a means of relieving pain during dentistry.
1844, Other Events	Future Tombstoner Nellie Cashman is born in Ireland. She will become known as "The Queen Of The Camp".		
1845, September 25	Martha Elizabeth Earp, sister to Wyatt Earp is born in Hartford KY. She dies a few months later.		
1845, July		An article credited to John L. O'Sullivan, the editor of the expansionist magazine, The United State Magazine uses the word "manifest destiny" for the first time. "Manifest Destiny" will become the mantra for so many settlers, miners, farmers, and federal legislation over the next 50 years.	
1845, October 4	Sarah Ann Harris Behan, wife of Peter Behan gives birth to their son, future Cochise County Sheriff, John Harris Behan.		

Date	Tombstone Events	Other Old West Events	Events Elsewhere
1845, October 10			The naval academy at Annapolis is opened.
1845, December			Edgar Allan Poe publishes his now-famous poem, "The Raven".
1846, January 25		Future Temperance Movement maven Carrie Nation is born. She will later make her mark on history by smashing barrels of whisky in an attempt to rid the populace of liquor.	
1846, June 19			The first baseball game occurs in the United States between the New Yorkers and the Knickerbockers in Hoboken, NJ. The New Yorkers won 23-1.
1846, September 10			Elias Howe patents the sewing machine.
1846, December 11	U.S. soldiers camped near what will become Tombstone are attacked by wild long-horn bulls.		
1846, December 25	Future Cochise County Deputy Sheriff under John Behan, William Milton Breakenridge is born in Watertown, NY.		
1847, February 11			Future inventor Thomas Edison is born.
1847, July 24		Mormon leader Brigham Young establishes Salt Lake City and the State of Deseret which is now Utah.	
1847, September 5		Future outlaw Jesse James is born in Missouri.	
			The State Of New Hampshire passes a law that limits workers to a 10-hour work day. Prior to this, both adults and children worked 12 hours or more a day in the textile mills along the Merrimack River.
1848, January 24		James Marshall discovers gold at John Sutter's mill near what is now Sacramento, CA setting off one of the biggest human migrations in history.	
1848, March 3	Robert Findley McLaury, better known as Frank McClaury is born in Korthright, New York.		
1848, March 19	Wyatt Earp is born to Nicholas Porter and Virginia Ann Earp in Monmouth, IL.		

Date	Tombstone Events	Other Old West Events	Events Elsewhere
1848, April		With a growing population in the west, the Pacific Mail Steamship Company is formed to deliver mail via the Isthmus Of Panama to the country's west coast.	
1848, July 4			Work begins on the Washington Monument in Washington, DC. It will take 36 years to complete being dedicated on February 21, 1885.
1848, July 19			The First Women's Right's Convention is held in Seneca Falls, NY. This made Lucretia Mott and Elizabeth Cady Stanton icons for the women's movement.
1848, December 29			Gas lighting is installed in The White House.
1848, Other Events		It takes about 3 months to go from New York to San Francisco via ship to Panama, across the isthmus, then via ship to San Francisco.	Chewing gum is invented. Karl Marx issues the *Communist Manifesto*.
1849, January			Amelia Bloomer begins publishing , "The Lily" a magazine about woman's rights and invents the piece of women's clothing that bears her name.
1849, January 4	Alvira Packingham Sullivan is born. She will later become the wife of Virgil Earp.		
1849, February 28		The first gold seekers arrive in San Francisco aboard the ship, "California". The population will swell to over 100,000 over the next 11 months.	
1849 Other events	Camillus Sidney Fly aka C.S. Fly is born. He will go on to be Tombstone's most famous photographer and Cochise County Sheriff.		What will become the Waltham Watch Company is founded in Roxbury, Massachusetts. In Rochester, New York, Margaret and Kate Fox found the spiritualism movement. The séance becomes a national pastime. Morgan Earp will later become fascinated with spiritualism.
1850, May 3	Future cow-boy, John Peters Ringo, better known as Johnny Ringo is born in Wayne County, Indiana.		

Date	Tombstone Events	Other Old West Events	Events Elsewhere
1850, September 28			Congress abolishes flogging as punishment in the Navy. Yet, teachers may still legally swat their young charges.
1850, August 26	Future Tombstone diarists George Whitwell Parsons is born is Washington, DC. His well-kept diary will serve as source material for Earpanians and other historians for years.		
1850, Other Events	Future Tombstone boarding house operator Nellie Cashman emigrates to the US from Ireland. She is 6 years old. Her family settles, not surprisingly, in Boston with many other Irish immigrants.		
1851, April 24	Morgan Earp, brother to Virgil and Wyatt, is born in Pella, IA.		
1851, June 2			The State Of Maine passes a law prohibiting the manufacture and sale of intoxicating beverages.
1851, June 9		San Francisco's population is growing quickly and along with it, the crime rate. Citizens are encouraged to enforce laws leading to the concept of Vigilante-ism.	
1851, August 14	Future dentists and Earp confidante, Doc Holliday is born into the southern aristocracy at Griffin, Georgia, just south of Atlanta.		
1851, September 1	Future Tombstone mayor, newspaperman, and Earp-supporter, John Phillip Clum is born in upstate New York near Claverack.		
1851, September 18			The New York Times debuts.
1851, Other events			Herman Melville publishes Moby Dick.
1852, March 13			The now-famous "Uncle Sam" caricature is drawn by Thomas Nast and first seen in a political cartoon. Nast would also create the traditional image of Santa Claus with his red suit and snowy-white beard.
1852, March 18		Wells Fargo & Company is officially organized.	
1852, March 21	John "Doc" Holliday is christened in Griffin Georgia.		

17

Date	Tombstone Events	Other Old West Events	Events Elsewhere
1852, April 13			Five & dime giant F.W. Woolworth is born.
1852, July 3			Congress acts to establish a United States mint in San Francisco.
1852, July 13		Wells-Fargo opens its California office in San Francisco.	
1852, October 13		Socialite and actress Lilly Langtry is born Emilie Charlotte LeBreton on the island of Jersey in the British Channel Islands, hence the later sobriquet "Jersey Lilly". She will later become the object of Judge Roy Bean's affections.	
1853, March 29			Work begins on the Capitol Building in Washington, DC.
1853, April 6		Ground is broken for the Mormon's temple at Salt Lake City.	
1853, June 30	Brother to Frank McLaury and also a future cow-boy, Thomas Clark McLaury, better known as Tom McLaury is born in Korthright, New York.		
1853, November 27		Bat Masterson is born.	
1853, December 30		James Gadsden signs a treaty with Mexico to buy 29,640 square miles, known as the "Gadsden Purchase", greatly adding to the land wealth of the US.	
1853, Other events			Policemen in New York City begin wearing uniforms to better identify themselves. Other major cities will soon follow.
1854, March 4		Sam Colt receives an order for 4,000 Model 1851 Navy revolvers from London's Board Of Ordnance.	
1854, August 29	Frederick James "Fred" Dodge, future gambler and Wells Fargo undercover agent is born in Spring Valley, CA.		
1854, Other Events	Tombstone correspondent to the San Diego Union, Clara Spaulding Brown, is born in New Hampshire.		

18

Date	Tombstone Events	Other Old West Events	Events Elsewhere
1855, March 3			Secretary of War, and future Confederate President, Jefferson Davis authorizes the introduction of camels to the southwestern US eventually leading to the formation of the US Army Camel Corps.
1855, March 9	Warren Earp, brother to Virgil, Wyatt and Morgan is born in Pella, IA.		
1855, December 23	Future Tombstone physician and businessman George Emory Goodfellow is born in Downieville, California.		
1855, Other events	Alice "Strallus" Parsons, sister to George W. Parsons is born. The two will remain close their entire lives. He will mention her often in his now-famous diary.	A Wells Fargo Stage is robbed for the first time. Over it's history, Wells Fargo Stages will be robbed 313 times for a total of $415,000. With the advent of Wells Fargo detectives, 240 stage robbers are convicted and 34 robberies are prevented.	About 400,000 immigrants arrive in New York this year.
1856, January 1			The use of postage stamps is now obligatory.
1856, April 21			The first railroad bridge opens across the Mississippi River connecting Davenport, Iowa and Rock Island, Illinois.
1856, August 19			Gail Borden patents condensed milk.
1856, Other events			The Western Union Telegraph Company is established.
1857, March 29		The Francher wagon train leaves Arkansas for California.	
1857, September 7		Paiute Indians attack the Francher wagon train a few days east of Salt Lake City, non-Mormons being viewed as a common enemy of the Indians and Mormons. Moreover, members of the train boasted of killing Mormon founder Joseph Smith. Then Mormon leader Brigham Young ordered his lieutenant, John D. Lee to finish off the emigrants leaving no trace for the oncoming U.S. Army, bent on squelching the Mormon's polygamous way of life. In all, 120 emigrants were killed. Any child under the age of five was spared and adopted by Mormon families.	
1857, Other Events			Future entertainer and funny-man Eddie Foy is born.

Date	Tombstone Events	Other Old West Events	Events Elsewhere
1858, February 28	Sister to James, Virgil, Wyatt, and Morgan Earp, Virginia Ann Earp is born in Pella, Iowa.		
1858, March 22		James Butler "Wild Bill" Hickok is elected constable of Monticello Township in Kansas.	
1858, September		Gold is discovered in the Kansas Territory about 90 miles from Pike's Peak in an area that is part of present-day Colorado.	
1858, October 9		The first Overland Mail stage arrives in St Louis from San Francisco making the trip in 23 days, 4 hours. Another stage running in exactly the opposite direct made the trip in 24 days, 20 hours.	
1858, October 27			Future president, also known as the western president, Theodore Roosevelt is born.
1858, December 25		"Uncle Dick" Wooten opens a tent saloon in Denver. To entice customers he treats the town to an entire barrel of "Old Towse" liquor. It is the first "big drunk" in Denver.	
1858, Other events	From *The Arizona Citizen* November 29, 1879 No Paper To-Morrow Owing to the short supply of rations in THE CITIZEN commissary department, our time will be principally occupied to-morrow in rustling provisions for a big dinner, and hence we beg our patrons to allow us, for once, the privilege of a national holiday.		Frederick Law Olmstead begins work to design Central Park in New York City. In Chicago, George Pullman begins building the railroad sleeping cars which will become synonymous with his name. Future Civil War photographer Matthew Brady sets up photography studios in New York and Washington. A financial panic grips the nation as business after business fails.
1859, August 27			The first commercial oil well is established in Pennsylvania.
1859, Other events			What will become the Great Atlantic and Pacific Tea Company, better known to most the A&P Store begins business as a general store in New York City.

Date	Tombstone Events	Other Old West Events	Events Elsewhere
1860, March 6		Christopher Spenser is granted a patent for his repeating rifle design. The Spenser rifle will become popular in the west.	
1860, April 3		Answering a need for faster mail delivery in the west, the Pony Express begins operations.	
1860, October 21	William Floyd Claiborne, better known as "Billy The Kid" Claiborne is born. His claim to fame will be that he was present at the OK Corral on October 26, 1881 but left before the shooting started.		
1860, November 21		Future "stock detective" and hired-killer, Tom Horn born.	
1861, April 12			The Civil War begins as South Carolina forces fire on Fort Sumter.
1861, June 16	Sister to James, Virgil, Wyatt, Morgan, and Virginia Ann Earp, Adelia Douglas Earp is born in Pella, Iowa.		
1861, July 26			Samuel Clemens aka Mark Twain heads west as assistant to his brother Orion, who is now the secretary of Nevada Territory.
1861, September 21	Virgil Earp marries Ellen Donahoo in Knoxville, Iowa.		
1861, October 4			Construction is authorized by the US Navy for an armored warship; the Monitor.
1861, November 20		The ill-fated Pony Express ends operation after only 19 months of service. It is made obsolete by the telegraph service.	
1861, Other Events	Josephine Marcus is born in New York City. She will become Mrs. Wyatt Earp and Wyatt will forever refer to her as "Sadie".	The dime novel, a small, almost comic-book type of publication insofar as its size and physical format, is born and quickly becomes popular entertainment. This medium will soon make heroes of Wild Bill Hickok and others.	
1862, March 7		Civil War guerilla-fighter, William Quantrill raids Aubrey, Kansas.	
1862, July 6			Samuel Clemens begins writing articles for the Territorial Enterprise, Virginia City's newspaper. He begins signing his article, Mark Twain.

Date	Tombstone Events	Other Old West Events	Events Elsewhere
1862, July 26	Fifteen days after his 19th birthday, Virgil Earp enlists in the Illinois Infantry to fight in the Civil War.		
1862, November 6			Transcontinental communication is made possible with the completion of the San Francisco to New York telegraph line.
1862, Other Events	Charlie Hoxie is born. He will partner with Wyatt Earp in the Dexter saloon in Alaska around 1900.		
1863, January 1			President Lincoln issues the Emancipation Proclamation freeing the slaves.
1863, February 24		Arizona becomes a U.S. Territory formed from part of the New Mexico Territory.	
1863, March 3		The Idaho Territory is formed. President Lincoln signs into law the first military draft known as the National Conscription Act. Prior to this time, the military depended on volunteers and state militia.	
1863, October 3			President Lincoln makes Thanksgiving a national holiday.
1863, July 13			The first military draft in the U.S. sparks riots in New York.
1863, August 21		Missourians William Quantrill, Bloody Bill Anderson, future outlaws Frank James and Cole Younger and 450 others attack the town of Lawrence, Kansas in one of the bloodiest guerrilla battles of the Civil War. 183 men and boys are killed and 185 homes and businesses burned.	
1864, February 17			In the first ever submarine attack the Southern submersible, H.L. Hunley sinks a Federal ship in Charlestown Harbor but goes down with all hands.

22

Date	Tombstone Events	Other Old West Events	Events Elsewhere
1864, November 29	Future Cochise County Deputy Sheriff (to Johnny Behan) Billy Breakenridge joins Chivington at Sand Creek.	Colonel John Chivington and 700 army volunteers attack Cheyenne Indian Black Kettle and his followers at Sand Creek in Colorado brutally murdering and scalping 100 men, women and children. At first, Chivington is lauded for his efforts to rid the west of the red man. When regular army officers visit the site, the murderous truth becomes known prompting investigation by the Congress and Army. By the time the investigations were concluded, Chivington was a civilian and beyond the reach of the military. He was never punished for what President Ulysses S. Grant termed as murder.	
1864, December 17	An Earp wagon train from Iowa headed for the San Bernardino Valley reaches the Cajon Pass.		
1864, Other events			"In God We Trust" appears for the first time on US currency. Union prisoners of war are sent to Andersonville Prison in Georgia, one of the most notorious prisoner of war camps ever with thousands dying of disease and starvation.
1865, April 9		General Robert E. Lee surrenders to Grant at Appomattox Court House in Virginia effectively ending the Civil War.	
1865, April 14			President Lincoln is mortally wounded while attending a play at Ford's Theatre. The perpetrator, John Wilkes Booth, is from a family of actors.
1865, April 26			John Wilkes Booth is shot to death near Bowling Green, Virginia.
1865, April 27			The steamship Sultana explodes on the Mississippi River killing 1700 people, mostly Union soldiers returning home from Confederate prisons.
1865, May 10		Guerrilla leader William "Bloody Bill" Quantrill is killed by Union soldiers near Louiseville, KY. He is only 27 years old.	

Date	Tombstone Events	Other Old West Events	Events Elsewhere
1865, June 26	Virgil Earp is discharged from the military.		
1865, July		Mormon leader Brigham Young takes his 50th bride.	
1865, Summer	17 year old Wyatt Earp (some sources say this was actually his brother, Virgil) gets a job driving stage between San Bernardino and Los Angeles – it is a 6 hour trip each way – Wyatt makes one round trip each day.		
1865, September 12	Newton Jasper Earp marries Nancy Jane Adamas at Philadelphia, MO and settles in Lamar, Missouri. They will have 5 children, most notably: Wyatt Clyde born August 25, 1872, most likely the first Earp to be named Wyatt in honor of his future-famous uncle and Virgil Edwin, born April 19, 1880, named for his future-famous uncle and the Earp who appeared on a game show in the 1950's.		
1865, December 24			The Ku Klux Klan is formed in Tennessee and begins the harassment of blacks.
1865, Other events			Beards become fashionable and mail is delivered free in larger cities. With the end of the Civil War, interest in baseball flourishes.
1866, March 6		William F. Cody, better known as Buffalo Bill Cody marries Louisa Frederici in St. Louis.	
1866, May 16			Congress authorizes a new coin; the nickel.
1866, April 13		Robert Leroy Parker is born at Beaver, Utah. He will later be known as Butch Cassidy.	
1866, July			A national currency is established.
1866, Other events		The era of the cattle-drive begins giving birth to the traditional "cowboy".	
1867, January 25		The February issue of *Harper's Weekly* publishes the first article about Wild Bill Hickok. Between Harper's and the dime novels, he will become a legend in his own time and a victim (see July 31, 1867) of his own fame.	

24

Date	Tombstone Events	Other Old West Events	Events Elsewhere
1867, March 2		The James Gang attempt to rob a bank in Savannah, Missouri. They shoot the bank president and leave empty-handed.	
1867, March 7			The Reconstruction Act is passed giving way to military rule of the South for the next ten years.
1867, March 30	From *The Arizona Citizen*, November 29, 1879 **WAGONS, WAGONS** **THE BEST IN THE MARKET** **JUST RECEIVED,** A LARGE NUMBER OF THOSE EX-CELLENT WAGONS manufactured by the **Fish Brothers** of Racine, Wis, AND FOR SALE BY L. Zeckendorf & Co. Tucson, Arizona **SOLE AGENTS FOR THIS TERRITORY**		Secretary of State William Seward purchases Alaska from Russia for $7.2 million. It instantly becomes known as Seward's folly. It will take 30 years, and the discovery of gold in that area for Americans to realize what a bargain this property really was.
1867, July 17			The first U.S. dental school is established at Harvard. The practice of dentistry is still very young when Doc attends the Pennsylvania College Of Dental Surgery in 1871.
1867, July 31		Wild Bill Hickok loses an election for town constable in Ellsworth, Kansas. Perhaps, because of his new-found fame (see January 25, 1867) the townspeople do not want to attract those who would come to challenge Wild Bill to a street fight.	
1867, November 25			Alfred Nobel patents his invention, dynamite. In 1896 his will establish the initial fund for what will become known as the Nobel Prize.
1868, March 12		The James-Younger Gang rob a bank in Russellville, Kentucky making off with $12,000.	
1868, May 3		Frontiersman Kit Carson dies.	
1868, July 25			Wyoming Territory is established.
1868, October 21			A major earthquake hits San Francisco.
1869, February 2			James Oliver patents an improved iron plow with a removable cutting edge allowing the edge to be periodically sharpened. It allows more efficient farming of the extremely tough mid-western sod.

Date	Tombstone Events	Other Old West Events	Events Elsewhere
1869, March	Future Cochise County Sheriff John Behan marries Victoria Zaff in Prescott, A.T.		
1869, April 5			Daniel F. Bakeman, last surviving soldier of the American Revolution dies at 109 years old.
1869, April 24		Wild Bill Hickok is elected sheriff of Hays, Kansas.	
1869, May 10		The Central Pacific Railroad line and the Union Pacific meet at Promontory Point, Utah to complete the first trans-continental rail line marking a major step in the development of the west.	
1869, July 13			Riots against the Chinese erupt in San Francisco. The growing number of Chinese works well and hard for little money becoming formidable competition for other laborers. Anti-Chinese sentiment will continue to grow in the west.
1869, Other Events	Spurred by the death of his mother and his profound feeling of loss, George W. Parsons begins what has become a world-famous diary chronicling his thoughts and adventures as he traveled to Tombstone, and other points if interest in the Old-West. He will keep his diary until 1929. Josephine Marcus, future wife of Wyatt Earp, moves with her family from New York to San Francisco. She is 8 years old.	It takes almost 8 days to go from New York to San Francisco via rail.	Work begins on New York's Brooklyn bridge.
1870, February 9			The first national Weather Bureau is established by an act of Congress as part of the Army Signal Corps. Future Tombstone Mayor John Clum will serve the Weather Bureau on his first trip west.
1870, March 3	Wyatt Earp is elected constable of the newly incorporated Lamar, Missouri.		
1870, July 24			The first railroad car to have traveled from San Francisco arrives in New York.
1870, September	Future Tombstone mayor, John Clum enters Rutgers College.		

Date	Tombstone Events	Other Old West Events	Events Elsewhere
1870, Other events			Future western actor William S. Hart is born.
1871, March 3	Wyatt Earp marries first wife Urilla Southerland. She will later die in childbirth.	The Indian Appropriations Act of 1871 essentially makes all Native Americans wards of the state forcing them onto reservations governed by various religious groups.	
1871, March 28	A warrant is issued for Wyatt's arrest for the theft of two horses from the Keys family in Indian Territory. History leaves only an inconclusive final account of the incident. Info courtesy Casey Teffertiller – *Wyatt Earp – The Life Behind The Legend*		
1871, April 15		Wild Bill Hickok is appointed Marshall of Abilene, KS.	
1871, May 1			The first US post cards are issued at a penny each.
1871, July 6	Victoria Behan, wife of John Harris Behan gives birth to their son, Albert. Following in his father's footsteps he would serve as a politician and lawman both as a Yuma Deputy Sheriff and US Deputy Marshal.		
1871, October	John Clum heads west to Santa Fe, New Mexico to accept a position as Observer Sergeant for the Signal Corps. The Signal Corp is essentially the National Weather Bureau. Clum is now – a Weatherman.		
1871, October 2		Mormon leader Brigham Young, a man with 50 wives, is arrested for polygamy.	
1871, October 8			Fire almost obliterates Chicago consuming 17,450 buildings in the great Chicago fire, purportedly started when Mrs. O' Leary's cow kicked over an oil lamp.
1871, October 24		Race riots erupt in Los Angeles against the Chinese.	The market price for beef in Texas is six cents per pound.

27

Date	Tombstone Events	Other Old West Events	Events Elsewhere
1871, December 30			An ad in the Boston Daily Advertiser reads: S.P. Bennett & Co. Men's and Boys Clothiers Overcoats - $15 to $38 Blue & Brown Beaver Suits - $22 Frock Coats - $17 Pants - $7 Vests - $7
1871, Other Events	Perhaps trying to escape into anonymity in reference to the horse-thieving incident in March of this year, Wyatt Earp earns a living buffalo hunting on the western plains.		
1872	Wyatt Earp meets Bat Masterson while hunting buffalo on the Arkansas River. The two will become friends for life.		
1872, February 20		From *The Arizona Citizen* November 29, 1879 The Telegraph The Sentinel says 1350 iron telegraph poles have passed Yuma consigned to Lieut. C. A. Booth, Maricopa. These metallic poles are to be used between Maricopa and Prescott and will place that portion of the line in excellent condition, so that when the Western Union line is completed to Tucson, we will have first-class telegraph communication.	The New York's Metropolitan Museum Of Art opens.
1872, March 1			Yellowstone Park is created by an act of Congress.
1872, June 12	Thanks to political strings pulled by his influential father, a prominent doctor and mining engineer from the California gold country, future Tombstone physician, George Goodfellow enrolls at Annapolis.		
1872, July	Nellie Cashman and her mother open a boarding house and restaurant for miners at Pioche, Nevada. This profession will eventually make her relatively rich, and famous.		
1872, November 15			The mayor of San Francisco exchanges telegraphic messages with a mayor in Australia marking the completion of a telegraph link between the US and Australia via Europe.
1872, December	George Goodfellow is forced to leave Annapolis in disgrace after being found guilty of fighting with a black student.		
1873, February 25			Singer Enrico Caruso is born.

Date	Tombstone Events	Other Old West Events	Events Elsewhere
1873, July 21		The James Gang robs the Rock Island Express and escape with $3,000.	
1873, August 1			What will become world-famous cable cars begin operating in San Francisco.
1873, August 8		Tucson vigilantes overpower US Marshal Milton Duffield and lynch four men.	
1873, September	George Goodfellow enrolls in the medical department at the University of Wooster in Cleveland.		
1873, September 18			The brokerage firm of Jay Cooke and Company falters marking a great financial panic throwing the country into a five-year depression.
1873, November	John Clum accepts an appointment as Indian Agent at the San Carlos Indian Reservation.		
1873, Other events	Wyatt Earp faces down Ben Thompson in Ellsworth, Kansas.	The Comstock Lode, one of the richest silver-ore finds in the world is discovered near Virginia City, Nevada. By the time the vein ran out, $135,800,000 worth of silver had been extracted.	
1874, January 5		School opens in Silver City, New Mexico. Among the first students at this public school is little Henry McCarty. He will later be known as Billy The Kid.	
1874, February 27	John Clum receives his commission as Indian Agent at San Carlos.		
1874, March 13		Un-enamored by show business, Wild Bill Hickok leaves Buffalo Bill Cody's wild west show. Hickok found it distasteful to parade about a stage imitating what he had done, and wanted to continue to do, in real-life.	
1874, March 24			Magician Harry Houdini born.
1874, May	Bessie Earp, wife of James Earp is charged with prostitution in Wichita, Kansas.		
1874, June 8		Apache Indian leader Cochise dies of cancer in the Dragoon mountains.	

Date	Tombstone Events	Other Old West Events	Events Elsewhere
1874, June 27		Bat Masterson and group of buffalo hunters hold off 700 Comanche, Kiowa and Cheyenne in 3 day Texas panhandle siege, later known as the "Battle of Adobe Walls".	
1874, August 8	Future Tombstone mayor, John Clum arrives at the San Carlos Indian Reservation. He is 23 years old and placed in charge of 700 Apache Indians who expressed their distaste of white man's rule by killing an Army Lieutenant and the former Indian Agent less than a year before. He vows that his administration will be different.		
1874, Other events	Wyatt Earp is elected Marshal in Dodge City. (This date is also given as June 1876 (Chaffin))	Joseph Glidden, an Illinois farmer invents barbed wire. This simple device will change the future of the country whereas it is now simple and cost-effective to mark off one's land and restrict livestock to that property. Range wars will be fought and many will die over this simple strand of prickly wire. In other news of the open range – the buffalo is hunted almost to extinction in about a two year period – 1872 to 1874.	
1875, January	1400 Rio Verde Apaches are added to Clum's San Carlos reservation population.	From The Arizona Citizen November 29, 1879 And now a Yankee inventor has come to the front with a with a patent "Automatic Self Rocking Bustle" warranted to – but we can't go on. What on earth will they get up next? without blushing	
1875, January 1	Doc Holliday exchanges gunfire with a saloon keeper in Dallas, Texas. This will mark a turning point for Doc as he recklessly wanders through the west in search of a cure for his debilitating, consumptive state.		
1875, April 21	Wyatt Earp is hired as a Wichita, Kansas policeman.		
1875, June	Future Cochise County Sheriff John Behan divorces his wife, Victoria.		
1875, July 26		Charles Boles aka Black Bart robs his first stagecoach. He will go on to commit another 27 robberies netting some $18,000 from Wells Fargo stages.	
1875, August 1	Future Tombstone miscreant Pete Spence, aka Peter Spencer (real name thought to be Lark Ferguson) begins his life of lawlessness by stealing a horse at Live Oak Canyon, Texas.		

Date	Tombstone Events	Other Old West Events	Events Elsewhere
1875 November		Frank Bryant discovers gold near Deadwood, South Dakota.	
1875, December	With things going well at San Carlos, Clum writes the Indian Bureau requesting more operating funds and a larger salary for himself. His letter is ignored.	Wells Fargo Express officials note 31 robberies and attempted robberies in California for 1875. Thieves have netted $80,000.	
1876, January 12	A local Wichita newspaper reports that policeman Wyatt Earp almost shoots himself as his gun discharges while he sits in a saloon. The hammer of his gun was resting on live ammo.		Author Jack London is born. He will later join gold-seekers in Alaska.
1876, January 24		Bat Masterson is wounded in a Mobeetie, Texas gun-battle over a woman. He is wounded but survives and will walk with a cane the rest of his life, thus, the name "Bat".	
1876, February	Frustrated by lack of funds, for himself and his now thousands of Apache charges, John Clum resigns his post as San Carlos Indian Agent. His resignation is accepted subject to his replacement which is not forthcoming.		The first sardines are canned.
1876, February 24	George Goodfellow, now known as Dr. Goodfellow graduates with honors from the University of Wooster in Cleveland, OH.		
1876, March 5		Wild Bill Hickok marries Agnes Lake in Cheyenne, Wyoming.	
1876, March 10			Alexander Graham Bell's telephone is now a functioning dream-come-true. Bells tells his assistant, Mr Watson, "…come here, I want you!"
1876 April 2			National League Baseball plays it's first official game, Boston beating Philadelphia six to five.
1876, April 3		A California law is passed stating that it will pay $300 for the arrest and conviction of each person found robbing a stage or a train.	

Date	Tombstone Events	Other Old West Events	Events Elsewhere
1876, April 19	The Wichita police commission votes Wyatt Earp out of the police force.		
1876, May	Without word of additional funds, a pay raise for himself, or a replacement agent, a band of Chiricahuas are added to John Clum's San Carlos Indian reservation.		Marking the country's first hundred years, the Centennial Exposition opens in Philadelphia. It is open six months; long enough for 10,000,000 people to walk through, awe-struck. One of the main exhibits is a large building containing a display of American inventions from the past few decades including the telephone and the typewriter.
1876, May 18	Wyatt Earp is hired as a Dodge City, Kansas policeman.		
1876, June 15	Bat Masterson is hired as Dodge City, Kansas policeman. Wyatt and Bat are then made Deputy Sheriffs.		
1876, June 25		Lt Col George A. Custer and the 7th Cavalry comprising 188 men are wiped out at Little Big Horn.	
1876, July	Future cow-boy turned Earp supporter, Turkey Creek Jack Johnson quarrels with his two mining partners in Deadwood, SD. They march out to a cemetery where Creek allows them each to take a shot at him after which he shoots them both dead.		
1876, July 11		Wild Bill Hickok arrives in what will be his last boom-town, Deadwood, SD.	
1876, July 29	John Clum heads east to Washington, D.C. from San Carlos to visit with friends and family. He brings 22 Apache Indians with him and puts on shows along the way to help defray expenses. The show, however, do not go over well as Custer's defeat at Little Big Horn only a month earlier has turned public sentiment away from the Indians.		
1876, August 2		Wild Bill Hickock is killed by Jack McCall while playing cards in Deadwood, Dakota Territory. He is holding the now famed "Aces & Eight's" hand, also known as the dead man's hand.	

Date	Tombstone Events	Other Old West Events	Events Elsewhere
1876, August 3		Jack McCall is acquitted of all charges for the murder of Wild Bill.	
1876, August 6	Tombstone diarists George W. Parsons arrives in Los Angeles after traveling from the east coast via water routes and across Central America. He will find life there too primitive and move on to San Francisco.		
1876, August 24	Pete Spence is involved in the robbery of Seeligson Brothers Bank in Goliad, Texas.		
1876, September 7		The James-Younger Gang attempt and fail to rob the First National Bank at Northfield, Minnesota. Several gangs members are wounded or killed by alert townspeople. Those townspeople that aren't armed throw rock s at the fleeing outlaws.	
1876, September 19			Melville Bissell patents the carpet sweeper.
1876, October 20		The Oregon legislature enacts a law that will pay $300 for the arrest and conviction of each person caught robbing a stage or train.	The alarm clock is patented.
1876, November	The Indian population reaches 4500 at the San Carlos reservation including 100 armed Indian police. All is quiet and running smoothly under Clum's administration. But Clum continues to wait for word of more money for himself, and more supplies for his Indians.		
1876, November 4	Dr. Goodfellow marries Kate Colt of Meadville, PA.		
1876, November 8	John Clum marries Mary Dennison Ware in Ohio.		
1876, December	Dr. Goodfellow establishes a medical practice at Oakland, CA.		
1876, December 4		Jack McCall is again tried for the murder of Wild Bill Hickok. He is convicted and sentenced to hang on March 1, 1877.	
1876, Other events			Central Park is opened in New York City.

Financier and oil tycoon, John D. Rockefeller holds a monopoly on 95% of the oil refining business in the US. |

Date	Tombstone Events	Other Old West Events	Events Elsewhere
1877, February 16		The Montana Territorial legislature enacts a law paying $300 for the arrest and conviction of each person caught trying to rob a stage or train.	
1877, March		Camp Huachuca (eventually known as Fort Huachuca and Tombstone founder Ed Schieffelin's base of operations from which Tombstone is founded) is established near the Mexican border in Arizona Territory. Tombstone founder Ed Schieffelin is among the troops.	
1877, March 1		Wells Fargo & Co. announces that it will pay $300 for the arrest and conviction of each person caught trying to rob a stage or train. Jack McCall is hanged at Yankton, Dakota Territory for the shooting of Wild Bill Hickok.	
1877, March 9	This day's *Arizona Miner* states that Dr. Goodfellow has opened a medical practice on Cortez Street in Prescott, A.T.		
1877, April	Other Prescott citizens noted during this time were future Tombstone lawyer Tom Fitch, future Cochise County Sheriff John Behan, future Tombstone policeman A.G. Bronk and future Tombstone Marshal, Virgil Earp.		
1877, April 26	Wyatt Earp is in Deadwood, Dakota Territory. (circa- spring / summer)	The Nevada State legislature enacts a law paying $250 for the arrest and conviction of each person caught trying to rob a stage or train.	
1877, June 27		Outlaws rob the Deadwood to Cheyenne stage in nearly the same spot for the third day in a row.	
1877, June		Chief Joseph of the Nez Perce Indians is defeated by Colonel Nelson Miles and forced onto a reservation in Oklahoma. Silver is discovered in what will become the city of Leadville, Colorado. Among the hopefuls is future Denver financier, Horace Tabor. He will soon purchase the "Matchless Mine" which will produce thousands of dollars in silver but will, like so many other mines, eventually play out. Despite this, he will ask his wife, on his death-bed, to hold onto the mine.	

Date	Tombstone Events	Other Old West Events	Events Elsewhere
1877, July 2			The Janesville Gazette in Wisconsin advertises flannel suits for $8.50 and men's dusters for $1.00. Info courtesy of Joan Severa, author, *Dressed For The Photographer – Ordinary Americans and Fashion 1840-1900*
1877, July 14			Many railroad workers strike in retaliation for a recent 10 percent pay cut, the second since the start of the depression in 1873. Sympathetic strikes by workers in other industries grind US commerce to a halt.
1877, July	After many thwarted attempts to raise his own salary and secure more money and supplies for his now 5,000 Indian charges, John Clum finally succumbs to government bureaucracy and leaves the San Carlos reservation despite not having someone to replace him. Clum and the Indian Bureau are equally miffed at each other. The Indians are saddened.		
1877, August 23		Outlaw John Wesley Hardin is captured aboard a train in Florida.	
1877, September	Prospector Ed Schieffelin records his first mining claim in the Pima County courthouse. He calls it "Tombstone".		
1877, October	John Clum and other Arizona businessmen buy interest in a newspaper, "The Arizona Citizen" and open for business in Florence, A.T.		
1877, November		Bat Masterson is elected sheriff of Ford County, Kansas.	
1877, November	Wyatt Earp meets Doc Holliday and Big Nose Kate at Fort Griffin, Texas.		
1877, November 16	John Clum is admitted to the Pinal County Bar as a practicing attorney in Tucson. He considers the job dull after looking after a band of Apaches.		
1877, Other events			George Selden develops a 2 cycle "gasoline carriage". Despite being a patent attorney, he does not seek his own patent for his own invention. The fame and the glory will later go to Henry Ford.

Date	Tombstone Events	Other Old West Events	Events Elsewhere
1878, January	Future Tombstone cow-boys, Frank McLaury meets Billy Clanton. Frank works for Billy building corral fence.		
1878, January 16			Future cowboy star Harry Carey is born.
1878, January 30		A posse led by Bat Masterson arrests train robbers "Dirty Dave" Rudebaugh and Edgar West in Kansas.	
1878, February 16			The silver dollar is legalized creating a demand for silver.
1878, February 18		English rancher and merchant John Tunstall is killed in New Mexico effectively starting the Lincoln County War. This will bring "Billy The Kid" to prominence.	
1878, February	Ed Schieffelin and Richard Gird establish the "Graveyard" and the "Lucky Cuss" mines in the Tombstone District.		
1878, April	Ed Schieffelin and Richard Gird establish the "Toughnut" and "Contention" mines in the Tombstone District. Prospectors begin to converge on the area.	The rush is on for the silver in Leadville, Colorado.	
1878, April 9		Marshal Ed Masterson of Dodge City, Kansas is gunned down. Ed is Bat's older brother.	
1878, April 28			Silent screen actor Lionel Barrymore born.
1878, May 8	Wyatt Earp returns to Dodge City from Texas accompanied by Mattie Blaylock, his so-called second wife. Wyatt is appointed assistant marshal.		
1878, June 8	John Henry Holliday takes out an ad in the Dodge City Times. It reads: J.H. Holliday, dentist, very respectfully offers his professional services to the citizens of Dodge City and surrounding country during the summer. Office at room No. 24, Dodge House. Where satisfaction is not given, money will be refunded.		
1878, June 12	President Hayes appoints Crawley Dake U.S. Marshal for Arizona Territory. He will later become Virgil and Wyatt's boss.		
1878, July 3			Songwriter George M. Cohan born.

Date	Tombstone Events	Other Old West Events	Events Elsewhere
1878, July 31	Outlaw Bill Brazelton holds up a Tucson to Florence stage. John Clum is among the passengers but escapes unharmed.		
1878, August 19		Outlaw William Brazelton is shot and killed near Tucson, A.T. His body is placed on public display as a warning to other outlaws.	
1878, September	Pete Spence is arrested in Tucson, A.T. for the murder of William Creelon.		
1878, October 10	On her way to destiny in Tombstone, restaurateur Nellie Cashman arrives in Tucson.		
1878, October 11		Texas outlaw Bill Longley is hung after reportedly killing 32 men.	
1878, October 15			Thomas Edison establishes the Edison Electric Light Company in New York. Although he does not yet have a working incandescent lamp, he knows it is only a matter of time.
1878, October 20	Henry Woodworth Clum is born to John and Mary Clum. It is "Woodworth" who will later contribute to his father's fame by publishing his memoirs.		
1878, October 30	Pete Spence is acquitted in the Pima County Courthouse in Tucson for the murder of William Creelon.		
1878, November 7	Dr. Goodfellow is elected County Coroner and Virgil Earp elected Village Constable in Prescott, A.T.		
1878, December	Tombstone town sites are surveyed and streets marked. Toughnut, Allen, Fremont and Safford streets run east-west while streets numbered one through 28 run north-south.		
1878, Other events		In 1878, the silver mines of Leadville, Colorado produce over $2 million dollars in silver.	George Eastman begins the manufacture of photographic dry plate.
1879, February 10	In Tombstone, Allen Street lots sell for $5 apiece. The town has 40 cabins and a population of 100.	The first electric lights used in San Francisco are in the California Theatre.	

From *The Arizona Citizen* November 29, 1879

J. H. Mahoney, Esq. Special Agent of the Post Office department passed through Yuma en route to California. He was much pleased with the Tombstone District which he had just visited.

Date	Tombstone Events	Other Old West Events	Events Elsewhere
1879, February 22			The first F.W. Woolworth store opens in Utica, NY. The first sale is an advertised 5 cent fire shovel.
1879, March 1	John Clum establishes his second newspaper, a daily, "The Tucson Citizen" in Tucson, A.T. By his own admission, he did not intend to engage in journalism as a profession, but finds the power of the written word a great way to poke jabs at government bureaucracy in general and the Bureau of Indian Affairs in particular.	A bottle of beer on the western frontier sells for a dollar while in Ohio, now firmly established and no longer a western frontier area, bottles of beer sell for a dollar a dozen.	
1879, March 11		Congress passes a bill to restrict Chinese immigration. It is vetoed by President Hayes.	
1879, March 21			The E.T. Foote store advertises men's Stetson hats for $2.50 in the Janesville Gazette in Wisconsin. Info courtesy of Joan Severa, author, *Dressed For The Photographer – Ordinary Americans and Fashion 1840-1900*
1879, March 27	George Whitwell Parsons begins his famous diary.		
1879, April 7	Dr. Goodfellow resigns as County Coroner in Prescott, A.T.		
1879, April 14	Charles R. Brown establishes Brown's Hotel on the corner of Fourth & Allen Street in Tombstone.		
1879, April 17	A Post Office is established at Charleston, 8 miles from Tombstone on the San Pedro river.		
1879, May	Tombstone population: 468.	A census in Leadville, Colorado reveals 31 restaurants, 17 barber-shops, 51 grocery stores, 4 banks, and 120 saloons.	
1879, May 7		When the State of California is drafting a new constitution, they insert and accept a clause forbidding the employment of any Chinese laborers.	
1879, May 26	A Post Office is established at Millville, directly across the San Pedro from Charleston and just few miles from Tombstone. Being so close to Charleston, the Millville Post Office will close 1 year later.		

38

Date	Tombstone Events	Other Old West Events	Events Elsewhere
1879, June	Tom Corrigan opens the Alhambra Saloon in Tombstone.		
1879, July	Nellie Cashman opens the Delmonico Restaurant in Tucson.		
1879, July	Gus Bilicke opens the Cosmopolitan Hotel in a tent in Tombstone.		
1879, July 19	Doc Holliday gets into a shooting affray with Mike Gordon in New Mexico.		
1879, August 14	Nellie Cashman meets John Clum for the first time when she runs an ad for her Delmonico Restaurant in Clum's newspaper, the "Arizona Daily Citizen".		
1879, August 16		Arizona Governor John Gosper offers a bounty of $500 for every stage robber caught.	
1879, September	Wyatt Earp and Mattie Blaylock leave Dodge City for Tombstone.	Ute Indians turn on their dictatorial Indian agent in an ugly uprising. It is quickly subdued.	
1879, September 20	Tombstone photographer C.S. Fly marries Mary E. (Mollie) Goodrich. Each will become photographers in their own right.		
1879, September 26		Fire destroy the entire business district in Deadwood, Dakota Territory.	
1879, October	Dr. Goodfellow travels via stage from Los Angles to Tucson. Local newspapers note that traveling with him is the newly installed Arizona Territory United States Marshall, Crawley Dake.		
1879, October 2	Tombstone's first newspaper, "The Nugget" is born. Info courtesy Casey Teffertiller – *Wyatt Earp – The Life Behind The Legend*		
1879, October 20			Thomas Edison fashions a light bulb using a thread of carbonized cotton fiber. It lasts 45 hours.

39

Date	Tombstone Events	Other Old West Events	Events Elsewhere
1879, November	Wyatt Earp and Mattie and James and Bessie Earp meet with Virgil and Allie Earp in Prescott, A.T. They head out together to Tombstone arriving November 29. Virgil Earp receives a U.S. Marshal commission in Tucson. He now works for Crawly Dake. Tombstone's population is just under 1000.	In Leadville, Colorado, the Tabor Opera House opens for business. This will be the fore-runner to the larger and more noted Tabor Opera House in Denver.	
1879, November 4		Bat Masterson is defeated for re-election as sheriff of Ford County, Kansas.	
1879, November 19		Leadville, Colorado vigilantes hang a claim jumper and an outlaw from the rafters of the jail kitchen. It is reported that hundreds of would-be thieves and outlaws leave the following day.	
1879 December	Future mayor John Clum visits Tombstone for the first time where the O.K. Corral is under construction.		
1879, December 4			Cowboy and actor Will Rogers born.
1879, Other Events	Future Cochise County Sheriff Johnny Behan meets Josephine Marcus for the first time in Prescott, AT. (Chaffin)	The mines in Leadville, Colorado produce over $9 million in silver. This makes future Denver financier, Horace Tabor a very rich man in a very short time. Meyer Guggenheim, a pauper from Switzerland, together with partner R. B. Graham goes into the mining business. Their claim brings them a reported $1,000 a day in profits. But one has to be rich just to survive in Leadville. Due to the new-found wealth and driven partly by the rigors of freighting materials up to it's 10,000 foot elevation, the cost of living in Leadville is 4 times what it is Denver. Faced with having to farm with limited water, Colorado becomes the first state in the nation to enact official supervision for of water rights marking off the state into districts.	

Date	Tombstone Events	Other Old West Events	Events Elsewhere
1880, January	John Clum sells his interest in the "Tucson Citizen" and heads for Tombstone.		
	A one-room school-house opens in Tombstone.		
1880, January 16			Future cowboy movie star Tom Mix is born. He will live to be a pall bearer at Wyatt Earp's funeral.
1880, January 29			Future actor and funny-man, W.C. Fields is born.
1880, February	Tombstone's population reaches 2000.	From *The Arizona Citizen* November 29, 1879 The calendar for the November term of court at Prescott occupies and column and a half of very fine type. This ought to be an indication of lively times.	From the February issue of "Demorests Mirror Of Fashions, "A very great and radical change is taking place in fashion… and it will take perhaps half a century to fully develop." This is referring to the revolution in fashion for the masses brought about by the development of the paper pattern. Info courtesy of Joan Severa, author, *Dressed For The Photographer – Ordinary Americans and Fashion 1840-1900*
1880, February 17	Famed Tombstone diarist George Whitwell Parson arrives in Tombstone meeting Wyatt Earp for the first time. George is traveling with a friend, Milton Clapp, a fellow bank clerk. Both had lost their jobs a few months earlier when the San Francisco bank they were working closed. George and Wyatt will be life-long friends.		
1880, (circa) March	George W. Parsons become a member of the Inner Council Of 10, the governing body for the Committee Of 100, the Vigilance Committee in Tombstone dedicated to assisting law enforcement when necessary.		The American branch of the Salvation Army is founded in Philadelphia. The organization was originally founded in England in 1865.
1880, April 6	A Post Office is established at Contention City, a milling town along the San Pedro River, 3 miles north of Charleston.		

Date	Tombstone Events	Other Old West Events	Events Elsewhere
1880, April 19	Virgil Edwin Earp is born to Newton Jasper Earp, nephew to his more famous namesake, Virgil Walter Earp. Virgil Edwin will have his 15 minutes of fame when in 1958 he appears on the television quiz show, "The $64,000 Question".		
1880, April 20	Nellie Cashman moves to Tombstone and opens the "Nevada Boot and Shoe Store", on Allen Street. She will soon open the Arcade Restaurant and Cash Store for food and groceries. She will sell her Cash Store three weeks before it burns to the ground.		
1880, May	Wells Fargo establishes an office in Tombstone.	From *The Arizona Citizen* November 29, 1879 **Another Score For Shakespeare** Yesterday, we received the following dispatch: EDITOR CITIZEN: The citizens of Shakespeare send you friendly greeting. We are now connected with you by telegraph and hope soon to be by rail. (Signed) Wm. G. Boyle To which we have replied in the following words: Wm. G. Boyle: The good people of Tucson reciprocate your kindly greeting and congratulate the citizens of Shakespeare upon their rapid progression and glorious prospects. John P. Clum This is a simple illustration of the fact that energy and merit are sure to develop important results.	
1880, May 1	The Tombstone Epitaph newspaper is born, founded by John P. Clum. Clum detractors predict the paper's demise within 6 months. The paper is published to this day.		The rise of the department store concept in the east, mail order to the west, and mass produced clothing contributed to the emergence of national fashion trends. Prior to this time, fashions were very regionalized. Info courtesy of Joan Severa, author, *Dressed For The Photographer – Ordinary Americans and Fashion 1840-1900*
1880, May 12	A 19 year old Josephine Marcus (the future Mrs. Wyatt Earp #3) arrives in Tombstone checking into the Cosmopolitan Hotel. (some accounts state that she stayed at the San Jose House) Cochise County Sheriff and Earp nemesis, Johnny Behan, is instantly smitten with her beauty.		
1880, June	The Oriental Saloon at Fifth and Allen Streets opens. It will become one of Tombstone's favorite "watering holes".		Ehrlich's mail order catalog advertises two calico dresses, one for $1.70 and another for $2.25. Info courtesy of Joan Severa, author, *Dressed For The Photographer – Ordinary Americans and Fashion 1840-1900*
1880, July	The Tombstone Epitaph, starting as a weekly newspaper becomes a daily. The Epitaph sides with the Earp faction and rival paper Nugget with the cow-boys.	Thomas Gardiner starts the Arizona Quarterly Illustrated magazine – pride 25 cents. (Chaffin)	
1880, July 4	The first Tombstone to Benson stagecoach operated by "Sandy Bob" Crouch leaves Tombstone.		

Date	Tombstone Events	Other Old West Events	Events Elsewhere
1880, July21	6 government mules are stolen from Camp John Rucker A.T. Cow-boys Curly Bill, Pony Deal, Zwing Hunt and Sherm McMasters are believed to be the culprits.		
1880, July 22	The Occidental Saloon opens.		
1880, July 25	The McLaury brothers are confronted at their ranch by acting U.S. Marshall Virgil Earp and brother Wyatt about the stolen government mules. They agree to return the mules to army on the condition that the Earp's leave. Upon the appointed place and time when the mules were due to be returned to First Lieutenant J.H. Hurst, the cow-boys gallop past him, thumbing their noses at him and causing great animosity between the cow-boy clan and the Earps.	From *The Arizona Citizen*, November 29, 1879 **Taken In At Leadville** N.D. Clark is the President of the First National bank of Ravenna, O. Last month he went to Leadville on a pleasure trip. While there a man named Lewis made his acquaintance. Lewis, after he had known Mr. Clark for a week or so went to him with, "a peculiar case" that he had just found. He had met on the mountains just out of town a young man whom he had not seen in fifteen years. The young man had shot a rival in a love affair and struck out for the west but now, having dug up a great amount of gold , thought of returning to his old mother in Kentucky. In order to do so, the young man would have to sell some bullion. Would Mr. Clark buy? Mr. Clark did buy a gold brick worth $14,000 for $10,000 cash. Mr. Clark left for Chicago, arriving in which city he found that his brick of gold was a clever compound of copper and other metals, the value being 10 cents instead of $10,000.	
1880, July 27	Sheriff Shibell names Wyatt Earp Deputy Sheriff for Tombstone.		
1880, August 6	Future Tombstone saloon-keeper and killer, Buckskin Frank Leslie marries May Killeen.		
1880, September	The Grand Hotel opens on Allen Street near Fifth.		
	The C.S. Fly photography studio opens.		
1880, September 10	Alder Randall is elected Tombstone's first mayor and Fred White elected town marshal.		
1880, September 21	The Tombstone Epitaph reports, "Dr. G. E. Goodfellow lately with the US Army at Fort Lowell was among the arrivals by coach yesterday. The Doctor is casting about for a location in civil practice, and thinks highly of our thriving city."		
1880, October	Dr. Goodfellow rents office space in the upper story of the Vickers Building on Fremont Street and begins his practice.		
1880, October 7	Pete Spence places an ad in the Tombstone *Nugget* warning against anyone buying a portion of the Franklin mining claim stating that it was his property.		

Date	Tombstone Events	Other Old West Events	Events Elsewhere
1880, October 10	Doc Holliday engages in a dispute with Johnny Tyler in the Oriental Saloon. Oriental owner, Milt Joyce tried to break it up and gun play erupted. Doc was fined $20 plus court costs over the affair. It aligned Milt Joyce, a man of some political influence, against the Earp-Holliday faction.		
1880, October 28	Cow-boy Curly Bill Brocious gets drunk and begins shooting-up Tombstone. In trying to disarm Curly Bill, Marshal Fred White is shot in the groin area. The event takes place on the site of what will later become the Birdcage Theatre. (The Birdcage opened in December, 1881.) White will later exonerate Curly Bill saying it was an accident.		
1880, October 29	A lynch party wants to string-up Curly Bill for Fred White's shooting. Wyatt, Morgan and Virgil escort Curly Bill to Tucson for safe keeping.		
1880, October 30	Marshal White dies and Virgil Earp is appointed Town Marshal.		
1880, November	Dr. Goodfellow establishes a hospital in New Boston, just outside the Tombstone Village limits.		
	The town of Galeyville is established. It will become a favorite hang-out for the cow-boy clan from Tombstone.		
1880, November 2		Pat Garrett is elected sheriff of Lincoln County, New Mexico. He will later tangle with Billy The Kid.	
1880, November 15	John Behan is appointed Pima County Deputy Sheriff for the Tombstone area.		
1880, November 15	Ben Sippy is elected Town Marshal in a special election due to Marshal Fred White's murder on October 28.. Virgil resigns as assistant marshal. John Behan is elected Deputy Sheriff of Pima County.		
1880, November 17		The Chinese Exclusion Treaty is signed by China and the US permitting the US to restrict but not exclude immigration of Chinese laborers.	

Date	Tombstone Events	Other Old West Events	Events Elsewhere
1880, December	In Charleston, just a few miles from Tombstone, Wyatt Earp recovers a horse from Billy Clanton, which he had earlier stolen. It is a tense stand-off between Wyatt and his brother Warren, against cow-boy Clanton, but the Earps finally win.	The population of Los Angeles is 11,000.	
1880, December	Construction begins on a meeting hall on Fremont Street near Fourth. It will be named Schieffelin Hall in honor of Tombstone's founder, Ed Schieffelin.	*From The Arizona Citizen, November 29, 1879* Guess Tombstone is to have a brewery from the looks of goods that came in on Tuesday last consigned to B. Werfritz & Co. Ed Note: This became the Golden Eagle Brewery and eventually, The Crystal Palace Saloon.	
1880, December	Al Schieffelin, seeing the opportunity for riches and the easy life sells his mining interests for $625,000, while his brother Ed sells his for $1.4mil. At this time, a 30X60 foot lot on Allen Street costs $6,000, a good mattress is $6 and a shanty in Tombstone rents for $50 a month. A Winchester model 1873 rifle sells for $27.		
1880, December 14	John Clum's first wife, Mary, dies a few days after giving birth to daughter, Bessie. Bessie, herself dies shortly after. Diarist George Parsons notes that it is a sad day in Tombstone for everyone.		
1880, December 23		Pat Garrett and his posse capture Billy The Kid at Stinking Springs, New Mexico in the wake of the Lincoln County War.	
1880, Other events		The federal census lists 1.8 people per square mile in Colorado. By the definition of less than 2 people per square mile, Colorado is still a frontier area. Denver has a population of 35,000. The Colorado Coal and Iron Company is formed in Pueblo, Colorado to provide steel rails for the Denver and Rio Grande railroad. The company is valued at $10M.	Also in 1880, the Kampf Brothers in New York invent a safety razor marking the beginning of the end for barber-shop shaves. And a company called Sherwin-Williams produces house paint made to a standard formula. Future actor Leo Carrillo is born. He will become famous in his later years playing the sidekick Pancho to Duncan Reynaldo's "Cisco Kid".

Date	Tombstone Events	Other Old West Events	Events Elsewhere
1881, January	Tombstone begins installing gas lights along the streets. Soon, public buildings and homes will be lit by gas. Tombstone, Tucson and Yuma are connected via the Southern Pacific's telegraph. Cochise County is created with Tombstone the county seat. John Behan is appointed its first County Sheriff, a job that was also desired by Wyatt Earp and would forever be a cause of friction between them.	Pat Garrett is sworn in as Lincoln County, NM sheriff.	The business card of a Chicago dressmaker reads, "Lizzie J. Benson Seamstress and Dressmaker 176 W. Indiana Street, Chicago Terms 1.25 per day Work done at home or elsewhere as desired Orders by mail promptly attended to." Info courtesy of Joan Severa, author, *Dressed For The Photographer – Ordinary Americans and Fashion 1840-1900*
1881, January 4	John Clum is elected the first mayor of Tombstone. (Three other mayors preceded Clum but they were appointed.) He had not intended to run but friends led by diarist George Parsons put his name on the ballot when the Republican candidate pulled out at the last minute, they having no desire for the unpopular Democratic candidate to win. In the same election, Virgil Earp is defeated for the City Marshal position by incumbent Ben Sippy, a move voters will later regret.		
1881, January 14	Johnny-Behind-The Deuce, a local card-sharp shoots an innocent man in near-byCharleston and is arrested. A lynch mob forms and Charleston Constable McKelvey removes him to Tombstone where he, Ben Sippy, Wyatt, and Virgil Earp, and Johnny Behan fend off the lynch mob until the prisoner can be taken to Tucson. Conflicting reports say either Wyatt or Sippy took the lead in fending off the crowd. (Subsequent movies and other depictions show Wyatt facing-down the angry mob by himself. While it is possible that Wyatt faced the mob by himself, or with help from Virgil or Johnny Behan, it is not likely that Sippy played a lead-role in this event. See June 28, 1881).		

Tombstone Economy 1881

Miners in Tombstone make $4 per day, working six days a week. Board is $8 per week and a house rents for $15 to $25 per month. Some quick math reveals that about 1/3 of a miner's wages went towards housing, a little better than 1/3 went to food, and the another 1/3 left for other necessities of life.

46

Date	Tombstone Events	Other Old West Events	Events Elsewhere
1881, January 19	The first Catholic church services are held in Tombstone.		
1881, February	The Cochise County Hospital is established within Tombstone city limits. Dr. Goodfellow's hospital is no longer needed and is closed.		
1881, February 11			Phoenix, A.T. is incorporated with 1,780 residents.
1881, February 16	Dave Rudabaugh, a former Earp nemesis pleads guilty to mail theft in New Mexico and is sentenced to 99 years in prison.		
1881, February 19	Luke Short kills Charlie Storms over a card game in Tombstone.		Kansas prohibits liquor except for scientific or medicinal purposes.
1881, March 2		William Bonney aka Billy The Kid continues to write to Governor Lew Wallace looking for clemency.	
1881, March 9		New Mexico governor Lew Wallace resigns.	
1881, March 10		Track-layers of the Southern Pacific railroad meet those of the Atchison, Topeka and Santa Fe in Deming, New Mexico marking the connection of the second transcontinental railroad.	
1881, March 12	The Tucson Weekly Citizen reports that Peter Spencer, Tom Carrigan, and J.F. Hutton had "struck it rich" in a Tombstone silver mine.		
1881, March 15	The Benson stage is robbed. Eli "Bud" Philpot and Peter Roering are killed. Bob Paul escapes with his life. Wyatt Earp and Johnny Behan organize a posse.	From *The Arizona Citizen* November 29, 1879 **DENTIST** **T.S. HITCHCOCK M.D.S.** Has permanently located in Tucson for the practice of Dentistry in all its branches. And can be found at J.S. Vosberg's rooms, opposite the Post Office.	
1881, March 16	A posse sets out to find the Benson stage robbers. Included are Bat Masterson, Johnny Behan, Billy Breakenridge, Wyatt, Morgan and Virgil Earp, George Parsons and Dr. Goodfellow. Luther King is arrested and names Harry Head, Bill Leonard and Jim Crane as accomplices. Behan returns King to Tombstone where he allows King to easily escape. It is now quite evident that Behan is playing both sides of the law.		

47

Date	Tombstone Events	Other Old West Events	Events Elsewhere
1881, March 25	An ominous portent of the future, an article in The Tombstone Epitaph reads, "Water has been struck in one of the leading mines…" "…leaves little doubt as to the permanency of the flow."		
1881, April	Tombstone, now incorporated, boasts a population of 4,000.		
1881, May 11	The Tombstone City Council appoints Dr. Goodfellow Health Officer at $50 per month. He will care for the indigent sick.		
1881, May 21			The American Red Cross is founded.
1881, May 25	Curley Bill is shot through the neck by one of his own men at Galeyville. The bullet enters his neck and exits his cheek. Surprisingly, Curley Bill survives.		
1881, June 2	Wyatt Earp tries to cut a deal with Ike Clanton to give up Head, Leonard and Crane for the Benson stage robbery. Wyatt figures if he can give the impression that he single-handedly captured the robbers, he'll be a "shoo-in" for a much wanted law enforcement appointment.	Work begins on the famous Tabor's Grand Opera House in Denver. Horace Tabor has a mural of Shakespeare removed in favor of his own picture. Denver is becoming quite cosmopolitan.	
1881, June 6	Known as outlaws, Bill Leonard and Harry Head are killed while trying to rob a store in New Mexico causing Wyatt's scheme to backfire. Ike Clanton becomes deathly afraid that his cow-boy cronies will discover the deal he made with Wyatt over the Benson stage affair.		
1881, June 6	Virgil Earp is temporarily appointed Tombstone Chief Of Police while Ben Sippy takes a leave of absence.		
1881, June 7	Schieffelin Hall is used for the first time for a dance sponsored by the Irish League.		
1881, June 16		According to a newspaper report in Santa Fe, Billy The Kid has more friends than anyone in Lincoln County.	
1881, June 26	A major fire levels two square blocks in Tombstone including 66 businesses. Within two weeks, most will be rebuilt and back in business.		

48

Date	Tombstone Events	Other Old West Events	Events Elsewhere
1881, June 28	Ben Sippy does not return as Tombstone's main law enforcement officer and Virgil Earp is again appointed Chief Of Police.	Development of the Atlanta copper claim begins in Arizona.	
1881, July	A disgruntled miner writes the *Nugget* newspaper stating that instead of finding their el-dorado of riches, many men ended up washing dishes or other menial jobs, finding instead, their Helldorado. The name Helldorado stuck becoming a the title of a book later written by Cochise County law-man, Billy Breakenridge and the theme for Tombstone's annual old-west celebration.		
1881, July	Faced with a high number of abdominal gunshot wounds, heretofore thought untreatable by the medical profession at large, Dr. Goodfellow begins attempts at treating the wounds. Figuring that the patient is already considered dead by most physicians neither he nor the patient have anything to lose. Time will prove Dr. Goodfellow quite successful. Sunday dinner at The Occidental is 50 cents. A faro dealer makes $6 per 4 hour shift. A below-ground miner makes $4 per day and a "soiled dove" make 25 cents to $1 per person. Josephine (Sadie) Marcus finds her lover, Johnny Behan in bed with another woman. Josephine moves out of the house they shared and moves into the San Jose House on the corner of Fifth and Fremont Street (this is still a boarding house) and will live on her own until she takes up with Wyatt Earp a few months later.	A 19 year old Frederick Remington arrives in Montana. Feeling that the old west is already beginning to fade, he begins capturing pieces of it on canvas. From *The Arizona Citizen* November 29, 1879 Thos. Fitch Clark Churchill **Fitch & Churchill** Attorneys and Counselors At Law, Prescott, Arizona. Will practice in all the Courts of the Territory. Special attention given to cases in the Supreme Court, to mining law, and the perfection of titles to mines and land. Office in the Bank Of Arizona building upstairs.	
1881, July 1	The Tombstone Daily Nugget newspaper reports that due to the recent fire, the annual July 4th parade will be cancelled.		

Date	Tombstone Events	Other Old West Events	Events Elsewhere
			Historical newspapers provide a fascinating insight into their period; not only in the news provided, but also in the way it is related. On successive pages are bits and pieces from two additional newspapers, the *Kansas City Evening Star* of October 26, 1881 (which lets us know there were other things going on that day despite a very newsworthy day in Tombstone), and some interesting tidbits from the *Boston Daily Advertiser* of December 30, 1871.
1881, July 5	A drunk Big Nose Kate implicates Doc Holliday in the March 15 robbery of the Benson stage and subsequent death of Bud Philpot. Judge Wells Spicer issues a warrant for Doc's arrest whereupon Cochise County Sheriff, Johnny Behan effects an arrest only to have Kate later recant her story.		
1881, July 10		Frank and Jesse James rob the Sexton Bank in Riverton, Iowa.	
1881, July 14		Sheriff Pat Garrett ambushes and kills Billy The Kid at Fort Sumner, NM.	
1881, July 15		The James Gang robs the Chicago, Rock Island Pacific Railroad at Winston, Missouri. They make off with $600 and kill the engineer and a passenger. Billy The Kid is buried next to fellow young-guns, Tom O' Folliard and Charlie Bowdre.	
1881, July 17		Former mountain man, Jim Bridger dies at the age of 77.	
1881, July 19		Sitting Bull and a small band of Lakota Indians, the last to do so, surrender to US officials. They have spent four years in exile in Canada.	
1881, July 28	Pete Spence and John Roberts, a foreman for the John Slaughter ranch buy Vogan's Alley, a saloon and bowling alley.		
1881, August		Cattle drives, a main-stay of cowboy-ing since the early 1870's come to the end of the trail. The last cattle drive take place along the Chisholm Trail as land begins to be fenced in by it's owners. Over 2 million head of cattle have been driven along this trail since 1866. Only a month after his death, the legend of Billy The Kid begins as "The True Life of Billy The Kid" is published in a dime novel. Future Klondike gold-rush luminary and con-man, Soapy Smith operates in Denver hoodwinking unsuspecting tourists and miners in a con-game where he sells bars of soap for $5 each. He claims that bills of up to $100 are wrapped up in the soap's labels and the only way to find the bills is buy the soap.	

Date	Tombstone Events	Other Old West Events	Events Elsewhere
1881, August 3	The Tombstone Union newspaper goes out of business. (Ironically, this happens just two months before the OK Corral incident, the reporting of which could have been their claim to fame).		
1881, August 12			Epic film-maker Cecil B. DeMille is born.
1881, August 13	Newman Haynes "Old Man" Clanton, father to Ike and Billy Clanton, is killed in the Guadalupe Canyon massacre.		
1881, August 31		Noted outlaw Black Bart robs the Roseburg, Oregon-Yreka stage in California.	
1881, September	Nellie Cashman opens the Russ House Restaurant in Tombstone. She operates it for a few months then sells it.		
1881, September 5		The Tabor Opera House opens in Denver. Patrons pay the hefty price of $2 to see *Maritanna* performed by the Grand English Opera Company in the $650,000 theatre.	
1881, September 8	The Tombstone-Bisbee stage is robbed. Pete Spence and Frank Stilwell are named as robbers.		
1881, September 13		Prentiss Ingraham's Buffalo Bill novel, "Bison Bill – The Prince Of The Reins" and The Red Riders Of The Overland" begins serialization in *Beadle's Half Dime Library*, a dime novel book.	
1881, September 20			President Garfield dies of gun shot wounds received July 2 from a disgruntled office seeker. Chester A. Arthur succeeds him.
1881, September 23	Dave Rudabaugh escapes from a Las Vegas, New Mexico jail and heads for Mexico.		
1881, October	There are 66 saloons in Tombstone; 1 saloon for every 68 persons. By contrast, 1714 Boston saw 10,000 inhabitants and 34 taverns or 1 drinking establishment for every 298 people. Tombstoners loved to imbibe.		London population:3.3 million, Paris population: 2.2 million, Tombstone population: 4500.
1881, October 5	Mayor Clum, John Behan and Virgil Earp form a posse to track down hostile Indians in the area.		

51

Date	Tombstone Events	Other Old West Events	Events Elsewhere
1881, October 17	With things heating up between the Earps and the cow-boys, Morgan Earp is appointed Tombstone special officer.		
1881, October 23	Diarist George Parsons writes, "Rather monotonous. I hope this state of things won't continue long."		
1881, October 25	Doc Holliday and Ike Clanton get into an argument at the Alhambra saloon. It spills into the street but is broken up by Morgan and Virgil Earp.		Painter Pablo Picasso born.
1881, October 26 12:30PM	Having already been threatened once earlier in the morning by Ike Clanton, Virgil discovers Ike roaming Tombstone armed with a pistol and rifle. Virgil disarms Ike, slamming him over the head with a six-shooter and, together with his brother Wyatt, drags him off to Judge Wallace's court for a hearing. The weather in Tombstone is unusually cold for this time of year.	An advertisement from the *Kansas City Evening Star* October 26, 1881: Hosiery, Buttons and Merino Underwear at astonishingly low prices. We are forced to do this to make room for our increasing stock of zephyrs, crewels and laces etc. One lot of buttons, 10cents, worth 25. One lot or pearl buttons, 25 cents worth 50 and 75. merino underwear reduced 331/3 per cent. Ladies making their fall purchases will do well to attend this sale. Helen Osborn & Co. 713 Main St.	
1881, October 26 12:40PM	Ike Clanton and Wyatt Earp argue in the court house awaiting Judge Wallace. Each one wants to fight the other right there in the courthouse. Animosity is reaching a boiling point.		
1881, October 26 12:50PM	Judge Wallace arrives and fines Ike $27.50 for carrying weapons within city limits. Virgil is ordered to secure Ike's guns at a local hotel until he sobers up. Wyatt is fuming.		
1881, October 26 12:57PM	Wyatt steps out of the court house and is confronted by cow-boy Tom McLaury who tries to pick a fight. Wyatt and McLaury argue for a moment or two, Wyatt slaps McLaury, hits him over the head with his six-shooter, and walks away leaving McLaury in a bloody lump on the sidewalk.		
1881, October 26 1:17PM	Wyatt observes several cow-boys at Spangenberg's gunsmith shop buying ammo and loading their gun belts.		

Date	Tombstone Events	Other Old West Events	Events Elsewhere
1881, October 26 2:17PM	A crowd begins to gather at Hafford's corner on Fourth and Allen Streets. The word is a fight is about to happen. Between the Earps and the cow-boys. Oddly, some of the cow-boys best guns including Curly Bill and Johnny Ringo are not around.		From the *Kansas City Evening Star*, Wednesday October 26, 1881

In Kansas City a war rages between saloon keepers and Clergy members who want to close the saloons on Sundays. Ministers see it as a moral issue. "Saloon men" see it as a business issue. The Kansas City Evening Star quotes the Reverend S. B. Bell as saying, "I am informed that about four years ago, an effort was made by the officials to close the saloons on the Sabbath, but, for want of public support in the measure, the attempt was a failure and the saloon men were triumphant!" |
1881, October 26 2:28PM	Sheriff John Behan leaves Hafford's to disarm the cow-boys.		
1881, October 26 2:46PM	Virgil, Wyatt, Morgan, and Doc Holliday leave Haffords headed for the OK Corral to disarm the cow-boys.		
1881, October 26 2:47PM	In a hail of lead and gun smoke the Earps and cow-boys finally clash. 30 shots and 30 seconds later Virgil and Morgan are wounded. Doc receives a slight wound and Wyatt is unscathed. Frank and Tom McLaury and Billy Clanton lie dead. Ike Clanton fled the fight within the first few seconds screaming, "Wyatt, don't shoot me. I'm unarmed!".		
1881, October 29	Chief Of Police Virgil Earp is relieved of duty pending an investigation of the OK Corral incident. James Flynn is appointed acting Chief.		
1881, October 31	Judge Wells Spicer begins a hearing to determine the possible need for a full-scale murder trial.		
1881, November		Outlaw Bill Miner robs the Sonora stage in California. A posse later catches up with him and his 3 accomplices. He will serve 20 years in San Quentin prison leaving behind the "old-west" as he knew it.	
1881, November 7	Wyatt Earp and Doc Holliday are locked up pending the investigation. Virgil and Morgan debilitated by bullet wounds are too ill to be jailed. Friends take turns guarding them against cow-boy assassins.		
1881, November 23	Wyatt and Doc are released from their incarceration.		
1881, November 29	The OK Corral inquest is finally complete.		

53

Date	Tombstone Events	Other Old West Events	Events Elsewhere
1881, November 30	Judge Wells Spicer hands down his finding in the OK Corral inquest noting, "…the defendants were fully justified in committing these homicides – this is a necessary act, done in the discharge of an official duty…" thereby exonerating the Earps and Holliday. The cowboy clan is fuming.	Front page news from the *Kansas City Evening Star*, Wednesday October 26, 1881 **THE FLOOD** The Mississippi Still on the Rampage - Immense Damage at Burlington and Quincy – Gathering Corn in Skiff – Other High-Water Incidents-	
1881, December	Rumors and death threats abound against the Earps, Holliday, Mayor Clum and attorney Tom Fitch who defended the Earps. Reverberations from the OK Corral gunshots reach Washington. US President Chester A. Arthur warns Tombstone residents to clean up the lawlessness or martial law will be imposed.		
1881, December 14	The Tombstone/Bisbee stage is attacked. Mayor Clum escapes with his life and suspects his assassination was the reason for the attack.	Prentiss Ingraham publishes his latest dime novel. " Adventures of Buffalo Bill from Boyhood to Manhood. Deeds of Daring and Romantic Incidents In The Life Of William F. Cody, the Monarch Of The Bordermen".	
1881, December 15		Socialite Lilly Langtry makes her acting debut at Haymarket Theatre in London, causing a sensation by being the first socialite to do so. Black Bart robs the Downieville – Marysville stage four miles outside Dobbins, California.	
1881, December 21	The Bird Cage Theatre opens for business on Allen Street. It is an immediate success.		
1881, December 24		On his last Christmas Eve, Jesse James dresses up as Santa Claus fir his two children, Jesse Jr, 6, and Mary, 2.	Mark Twain publishes *The Prince and the Pauper.*
1881, December 28 11:30PM	Virgil Earp is ambushed and shot by unknown assailants as he walks across Allen Street at Fifth. His left arm is nearly severed. Friends bring him to the Cosmopolitan Hotel where Doctors Mathews and Goodfellow tend to his wounds.		Helen Hunt Jackson publishes *A Century Of Injustice* about the mistreatment of Indians. Frederick Ives produces the first color photographs.
1881, December 29	In the wake of Vigil's near-assassination, U.S. Marshal Crawly Dake names Wyatt Earp a U.S. Deputy Marshall and authorizes him to form a posse to pursue Vigil's would-be killers.		An electric probe is invented for finding bullets in the body. The Barnum and Bailey Circus is founded.

Date	Tombstone Events	Other Old West Events	Events Elsewhere
1881, December 30	Mining entrepreneur Dick Gird sells his Tombstone mining interests for more than $2, 000,000.		Denver is the fourth city in the US with electric street lights.
1881, Other events	Tombstone's population reaches 5,000.		
1882, January	Fred Emerson Brook replaces John Clum as Tombstone's postmaster. He will serve until January 1885.		
1882, January 3	Today is election day in Tombstone. John Clum does not run for re-election as Mayor. Local sentiment has turned against the once popular Earps and their allies in the wake of all the violence. John Carr, a local blacksmith and Irish immigrant is elected Tombstone's mayor. Dave Neagle becomes the new City Marshal.		
1882, January 17	Doc Holliday and Johnny Ringo exchange harsh words in the street. Reportedly, "I'm your huckleberry!" was Doc's reply to Ringo's call for a fight. Both are disarmed.		
1882, January 26		Black Bart robs the Ukian-Cloverdale stage six miles from Cloverdale, California.	
1882, January 29	25 year old Endicott Peabody arrives in Tombstone with the intent of building St. Paul's church. It was not above the young clergyman to walk into a saloon looking for donations for the church building fund. The gamblers contributed greatly to the church's $4653 cost. Peabody noted, "The Lord's pot must be kept boiling, even if it takes the devil's kindling wood".		
1882, February		Roller skating mania is reported in Kansas.	
1882, February 2			The Roman Catholic church permits the founding of the Knights of Columbus.
1882, February 9	Ike Clanton files a second murder charge against the Earps in Contention City. It is unsuccessful.		
1882, February 15	A third murder charge is filed against the Earps, this time in Tombstone. It too, is unsuccessful.		

Date	Tombstone Events	Other Old West Events	Events Elsewhere
1882, February 18		In New Mexico, Pat Garrett collects his $500 reward for ridding the populace of Billy The Kid.	
1882, February 26		Frederick Remington's first nationally published illustration titled, "Cowboys of Arizona" appears in Harper's Weekly.	
1882, March		Famed Indian fighter general George Crook arrives at the San Carlos Indian reservation to restore order. Crook writes that the Indians had all the reasons in the world to complain and had shown great restraint in not causing more trouble.	
1882, March 18	Morgan Earp is assassinated while playing pool at Campbell & Hatch's Saloon. The shot passes through Morgan and hits bystander George Berry inflicting a flesh wound. Wyatt Earp, also present is barely missed by a second shot. Several members of the cow-boy clan are suspected of the shooting.		
1882, March 19	Morgan's body lies in state at the Cosmopolitan Hotel, then is shipped to his parents living in Colton, California.		
1882, March 20 Morning	Wyatt and Virgil Earp along with their wives, several compatriots and Morgan's widow leave for Colton, California to be with Earp parents Nicholas and Virginia.		
1882, March 20 Evening	While boarding the train in Tucson, Wyatt meets Frank Stilwell, suspected of being one of Morgan's murderers. The next morning, Stillwell is found dead on the train tracks, riddled with bullets and buckshot. Wyatt and his party catch a freight train back to Tombstone.		

56

Date	Tombstone Events	Other Old West Events	Events Elsewhere
1882, March 21	The killing of Stillwell has put the Earp party in a precarious position. Although they are authorized as federal deputies to hunt down Morgan's killers and restore order to the area, County Sheriff John Behan and the Clanton cronies are now pursuing them for Stillwell's death. The Earp posse begins their pursuit of the rest of the cow-boy clan. This pursuit has come to be known as the "Vendetta Ride" or "The Last Ride Of Wyatt Earp and his Immortals".		Max Aronson is born in Little Rock, Arkansas. He will later be known as Broncho Billy Anderson and become not only the world's first western movie star but the first ever movie star when he appears in the first movie with a plot, *The Great Train Robbery* in 1903. He will receive an award in 1957 for his "contribution to the development of motion pictures".
1882, March 22	Florentino Cruz, a half-breed Indian and suspected accomplice in Morgan's murder is killed by the Earp posse in the Dragoon Mountains surrounding Tombstone.	From the *Boston Daily Advertiser* of December 30, 1871, the following quips are noted under the heading "In General" • Iowa has 48 resident Indians. • Nebraska has an editor who spells wife, yf. • Smoking is reported to be declining in England. • The bell worn by Mrs. O'Leary's cow is exhibited in 81 different places in Chicago.	
1882, March 23	The Earp posse fights a gun battle with members of the cow-boy faction at Iron Springs. A blast from Wyatt's shotgun nearly cuts Curley Bill in two, killing him instantly. Wyatt's hat and coat are full of bullet holes but, again, he is miraculously untouched.		
1882, March 26	Two masked men rob the Tombstone Mill and Mining Company killing M.R. Peel. Deputy Billy Breckenridge and his posse shoot it out with the bandits killing outlaws Billy Grounds. Outlaw Zwing Hunt is captured.		
1882, March 27	Cochise County Sheriff Johnny Behan collects a posse and rides out in search of the Earp posse, wanted for the killing of Frank Stillwell in Tucson.		
1882, March 28	The Behan posse arrive at Henry Hooker's ranch one day behind the Earp posse. Behan and Hooker trade angry remarks. Hooker is an Earp supporter.		

57

Date	Tombstone Events	Other Old West Events	Events Elsewhere
1882, March 29	While performing an autopsy on cattle rustler Billy Grounds, Dr. Goodfellow notes that some of the buckshot that had been fired into Ground's face had not penetrated a silk scarf worn around his neck. Later, in 1887 Goodfellow would write a paper, "The Impenetrability Of Silk To Bullets" which was published in the Southern California Practitioner.		An ad in the *Boston Daily Advertiser* of December 30, 1871 **YOSEMITE VALLEY** By the urgent request of many prominent citizens, clergymen, School superintendents, and others, Excursions to the wonderful scenes of Yosemite Valley, the Big Tree Forrest, and other remarkable places in California, will be resumed WEDNESDAY, Dec 27, 1871 Trains leave Tremont Temple at 2:30 and 7:00P.M. each day, Wednesday, Thursday, Friday, and Saturday, Dec 27, 28, 29, and 30. **J.M. Hutchings,** The old Pioneer and long resident of Yosemite - Conductor
1882, April	Former Mayor John Clum sells his Tombstone Epitaph newspaper and leaves Tombstone. The transfer of ownership to Sam Purdy occurs May 1, 1882, exactly two years after it's inception.		
1882, April 8	Wyatt, Doc Holliday and their posse arrive in Silver City, New Mexico. A newspaper reports that they are "armed to the teeth".		
1882, April 3		Bob Ford kills Jesse James just for the publicity. Eventually, Ford will be reviled while Jesse James enjoys notoriety.	
1882, April 13		Oscar Wilde lectures at the Tabor Opera House in Denver. Tickets are $1.50.	
1882, April 26	President Chester A. Arthur orders federal troops into Arizona to deal with the "cow-boy" problem.		
1882, April 30	Diarist George Parsons writes, "14 murders and assassinations in 10 days…more than one a day!".		
1882, May 3	President Chester A. Arthur threatens to declare martial law in Tombstone within two weeks admonishing "such insurgents to disperse and retire peaceably to their respective abodes".		
1882, May 5	The *Tombstone Daily Nugget*, Tombstone's first newspaper established in 1879, goes out of business.		
1882, May 6		Congress enacts the Chinese Exclusion Act excluding Chinese laborers for 10 years.	

58

Date	Tombstone Events	Other Old West Events	Events Elsewhere
1882, May 15	Doc Holliday is arrested in Denver, Colorado by a con man claiming to be an officer.		
1882, May 16	Doc Holliday is arrested in Denver for the murder of Frank Stillwell in Tucson. Arizona authorities will try unsuccessfully to extradite Doc for trial.		
1882, May 17	Doc's old friend, Bat Masterson obtains a writ of habeas corpus on Doc's behalf.		
1882, May 22	Wyatt Earp arrives in Gunnison, Colorado and wires to Josie in San Francisco. She replies asking Wyatt to meet her there.		
1882, May 25	Another major fire destroys a large section of Tombstone's business district. The building housing "The Nugget", now a former rival newspaper to The Epitaph is destroyed.	The Cheyenne Opera House in Wyoming, built at a cost of $50,000 opens for business.	
1882, May 29	Realizing that sending Doc Holliday to Arizona will mean his certain death at the hands of those who perpetrated a large amount of the trouble there, Colorado's Governor Pitkin, after a discussion with Bat Masterson, denies Holliday's extradition to Arizona.	From the *Boston Daily Advertiser* of December 30, 1871, the following quips are noted under the heading "In General" • A French geologist says the earth will not be consumed by fire but will break from intense cold. • John C. Calhoun's plantation in South Carolina has been bought by a wealthy colored man. • Tiger Tail, a son of the famous Seminole chief of the same name now peddles pumpkins in Key West.	
1882, June	Arizona authorities try to extradite Wyatt and Doc from Colorado to stand trial for Stilwell's death. Fearing conviction or their own murders Wyatt seeks help from Colorado authorities. Colorado refuses to recognize the Arizona extradition papers and they remain in Colorado. Wyatt will eventually travel to San Francisco to re-join Josephine Marcus. The Cochise County Board of Supervisors note that they have paid Dr. Goodfellow an enormous sum, $12,282 for his services caring for the indigent sick at the county hospital noting inconsistencies in his billing practices. Still, he is retained.		

Date	Tombstone Events	Other Old West Events	Events Elsewhere
1882, June 18	Tombstone's St. Paul's church is completed at the price of $5000. The first service is held with Endicott Peabody officiating.		
1882, June 20		Annie Oakley and Frank Butler are issued a marriage license in Windsor, Ontario, Canada although they were first married in 1876. The "second wedding" may have been prompted by Frank's divorce not being final at the time of the first wedding.	
1882, July	Wyatt Earp rejoins Josephine Marcus in San Francisco. (Chaffin)		
1882, July 11	Tombstone's Dr. Goodfellow rides out to Leslie's ranch to find a dead Molly Bradshaw and wounded James Neal.	The Denver and Rio Grande's extension of rails from Durango to Silverton, Colorado is completed.	
1882, July 13	Earp detractor Johnny Ringo is found dead of a single gun shot wound to the head a few miles out of Tombstone. He is found propped up in the fork of a large tree with his boots missing and a single round missing from his revolver. Whether it was suicide or not has been a point of contention ever since.	Black Bart robs the LaPorte-Oroville stage near Strawberry Valley, California.	
1882, July 17	Seminarian Endicott Peabody leaves Tombstone to pursue his dream of establishing a boy's school. His Tombstone legacy is St Paul's Episcopal church that stands today.		
1882, July 22		Arizona Territory US Marshal Crawley Dake resigns leaving a legacy of misappropriated funds that are only partially repaid by bondsmen.	
1882, July 23		Mormons buy 80 acres of land from Charles Hayden for $3,000 and Tempe, A.T. is born.	
1882, August 1		With hot mineral waters, thought to cure a number of ailments as it's claim to fame, the city of Glenwood Springs is established in Colorado. This will be the last town visited by Doc Holliday.	
1882, August 2		Judge Roy Bean is appointed justice of the peace for Pecos County Texas.	
1882, August 3		The Cheyenne Electric Light Company is formed in Cheyenne, Wyoming.	
1882, August 4		The first post office is established at Billings, Montana.	
1882, September			Future writer and "Klondiker", Jack London enters first grade.

Date	Tombstone Events	Other Old West Events	Events Elsewhere
1882, September 4			Thomas Edison begins supplying electricity to New York City from his own power station. The city begins to twinkle with incandescent light.
1882, September 10	Endicott Peabody's successor, Rev. J.T. Bagnall is ordained at St. Paul's church in Tombstone. He will preach at St. Paul's until 1884.		
1882, September 14		Black Bart robs the Yreka-Redding stage near Redding, California.	
1882, September 30		Colorado's lieutenant-governor and millionaire, Horace Tabor secretly weds Elizabeth McCourt (Baby Doe) three months before his divorce from his wife of 29 years in final.	
1882, October 5		Outlaw Frank James surrenders.	
1882, October 22		The Cheyenne, Wyoming telephone exchange lists 135 names.	
1882, November	Patriarch Nicholas Porter Earp is elected Justice Of The Peace in Colton, California.		
1882, November 6		British actress Lilly Langtry makes her American acting debut at New York's Fifth Avenue Theater in Shakespeare's *As You Like It*.	
1882, November 14	Billy "The Kid" Claiborne is shot by Buckskin Frank Leslie outside the Oriental Saloon at about 7.30 in the morning.. Claiborn is treated by both Drs. G.C. Willis and Goodfellow. He dies at the County Hospital.		
1882, November 18		Prentiss Ingraham's novel, "The League Of Three or Buffalo Bill's Pledge" begins serialization in the *Banner Weekly*.	
1882, December 11			Thomas Edison lights up the Bijou Theatre in Boston with his incandescent light bulbs – 650 of them.
1882, December 12		The Gila Bend Indian Reservation is established in Arizona for the Papago Indians.	
1882, December	Tombstone's population reaches 5,299, almost half the population of Los Angeles.		

Date	Tombstone Events	Other Old West Events	Events Elsewhere
1882, Other events	From the *Boston Daily Advertiser* of December 30, 1871, the following quips are noted under the heading "In General" • Why are washerwomen the silliest of people? Because they put out their tubs to catch soft water when it rains hard. • The jail at Waco, Texas was set on fire three times in as many days, recently, by the prisoners who preferred roasting to a longer stay in the vile place.	Belle Starr is sentenced to a year in a Detroit jail for horse theft. Robert Leroy Parker leaves his Beaver, Utah home. He will soon be known as Butch Cassidy. Future western artist Charles M. Russell works as a cowpuncher in Montana. Helen Hunt Jackson visits San Jacinto, California where she meets Indian Ramona Lobo who will serve as the model for her lead character in her 1884 novel, Ramona. Note: The Ramona Pageant, an event celebrating the story of Ramona and the book is held each year in Hemet, California.	The first Labor Day holiday is celebrated.
1883, January		Augusta Tabor, estranged wife of millionaire Horace Tabor wins a settlement from him in the amount of $300,000 in mining stock and their home. His marriage to Baby Doe is still a secret.	
1883, January 13		Prentiss Ingraham's "Buffalo Bill's Grip or Oathbound To Custer" begins serialization in *Beadle's Dime Library*.	
1883, January 22		In Nevada, Wells-Fargo messenger "Hold The Fort" Ross becomes a hero when thwarts repeated attempts by outlaws to raid the express car he is guarding.	
1883, February	Now working for the Postal Department in Washington, John Clum marries Belle Atwood. Former Behan associate and former editor of rival newspaper, "The Nugget" Harry Woods takes command of The Epitaph.		Clarence Edward Mulford is born. He will later create the character of Hopalong Cassidy.
1883, February 26		The Rocky Mountain Bell Telephone Company is established. It will serve Utah and Montana.	
1883, March 1		Colorado millionaire and politician, Horace Tabor, 52, and divorce', Elizabeth McCourt also known as "Baby Doe", 28, are wed in an opulent ceremony in Washington, D.C. Doe wears a $7,000 wedding dress and receives a $75,000 diamond necklace as a wedding present.	

Date	Tombstone Events	Other Old West Events	Events Elsewhere
1883, March 15		Lillie Langtry appears at the Cheyenne Opera House.	
1883, March 24			Telephone operation is established between New York and Chicago.
1883, March 26		Cowboys work the range for $25 per month.	Defining "conspicuous extravagance" William K. Venderbilt throws a dress ball for New York's high society. It costs $250,000.
1883, April		Annie Oakley and husband Frank Butler join the Sells Brothers Circus.	
1883, April 1		Texas cowboys strike for higher wages. The strike is soon broken and the cowboys go back to work for $25 per month.	
1883, April 12		Black Bart robs the Lakeport-Cloverdale stage near Cloverdale, California.	
1883, May	A Yaqui Indian from Mexico is brought to Dr. Goodfellow with a severe chest and stomach wound. The doctor treated the wound and the Indian recovered by August returning to Mexico.		
1883, May 1		In Omaha, William F. (Buffalo Bill) Cody stages the first Wild West Show.	
1883, May 16	A Post Office is established at Fairbank, about 9 miles west of Tombstone. Fairbank has served as a railroad supply point for Tombstone since 1882.		
1883, May 24			Begun in 1869, the Brooklyn Bridge is opened with great fanfare. Officiating the event are President Chester A. Arthur and Governor Grover Cleveland. New Yorkers are convinced it is the eighth wonder of the world.
1883, May 26		"Wild Bill, the Whirlwind of the West" begins serialization in *Beadles Weekly*.	
1883, June 5	Coming to the aid of Luke Short in his differences with the mayor of Dodge City, Wyatt Earp, Bat Masterson, Charlie Bassett and others have their now famous picture taken as the "Dodge City Peace Commission".		

63

Date	Tombstone Events	Other Old West Events	Events Elsewhere
1883, June 23		Black Bart robs the Jackson-Ione stage near Jackson, California.	
1883, July 4		Buffalo Bill Cody presents a circus of cowboys, Indians, sharp-shooters and others in North Platte, Nebraska. It will eventually evolve into his famed traveling Wild West show.	
1883, August		Wells-Fargo Company claims to cover 33,000 miles connecting "nearly every Hamlet, Town and City in the US and Canada".	
1883, August 12		Two Arizona stages are robbed in one night, the Prescott-Ash Fork and the Florence-Globe. One Wells-Fargo guard is killed.	
1883, September 13	Working for the Southern Pacific Railroad, Virgil Earp refuses to allow the tracks of the California Southern to cross the tracks of the S.P. in Colton. Then California Governor Waterman led the Sheriff and contingent of San Bernardino men in a successful coup against Virgil. It was said this was the first time an Earp ever backed down.		The trip that took Lewis and Clark over two years to complete can now be made in 9 days via rail and stage.
1883, October		The Northern Pacific Refrigerator Car Company opens for business in the Dakota Badlands.. They will raise and slaughter beef cattle on the plains and ship the meat east via rail in cars kept cold by ice taken from the Little Missouri River.	
1883, October 12		The Eastern Montana Stockgrower's Association is established.	
1883, October 17-20		Buffalo Bill's Wild west Show plays in Chicago.	
1883, October 28			Yellowstone National Park closes for the summer season after receiving 20,000 visitors.
1883, November 3		Black Bart pulls his last stage robbery, the Sonora-Milton stage near Copperopolis, California. He will leave behind a handkerchief with a laundry mark, which helps Wells-Fargo agent, James Hume effect his later capture in San Francisco.	

64

Date	Tombstone Events	Other Old West Events	Events Elsewhere
1883, November 17	Tombstone's population tops out at 6,000. (Chaffin)	After committing numerous hold-ups, Charles Boles aka Black Bart pleads guilty to one charge of stage-coach robbery and is sentenced to 6 years in San Quentin. As a model prisoner, he was released in only four years and again began his stage-robbing antics. By November, 1888 he had committed 3 more robberies. Wells-Fargo let it be known that Black Bart was the prime suspect. No doubt knowing that he would serve considerable time in prison if caught, Black Bart disappeared, never to be heard from or seen again.	
1883, November 18			The United States adopts Standard Time establishing four Time Zones.
1883, December	Tombstone mine offices and mills are linked by telephone.		
1883, December 8	Five men, thought to belong to the Clanton-McLaury Cow-boy gang rob the Goldwater and Castenada Store in Bisbee, AZ. Four citizens are killed in the ensuing melee. It becomes known as the Bisbee Massacre.		
1883, December 24	Belle Atwood Clum, wife of John Clum gives birth to a baby girl – Caro.		
1883, December 26		A bitter cold snap signals the beginning of a very tough winter.	
1883, Other Events	It is about this time that Wyatt Earp is purportedly presented with the now-fabled long-barreled, six-shooter by dime-novelist, Ned Buntline. Hence the name, "Buntline Special". The gun was supposedly given to Wyatt in exchange for information about people, places and events that he (Wyatt) knew about which Buntline would turn into dime novels. Some say this never occurred. Others (the movie *Tombstone*) have Wyatt using the pistol before he even received it. Only Wyatt knows the truth and he isn't talking.	Wells-Fargo is now operating 1,163 offices.	Life magazine is established. Ladies Home Journal is established. Robert Louis Stevenson publishes Treasure Island. Mark Twain publishes *Life On The Mississippi.* Thomas Edison demonstrates an electric trolley which derives it's electrical current from a third rail.

Date	Tombstone Events	Other Old West Events	Events Elsewhere
1884, January			Mark Twain publishes *The Adventures Of Huckleberry Finn.*
1884, January 8		The Denver Chamber Of Commerce is formed.	
1884, January 31		The Arizona pioneer's Historical Society is organized in Tucson.	
1884, February 22	John Heath is lynched by a Tombstone mob for his part in the "Bisbee Massacre". Although illegal, many of the area's prominent citizens approved of it. Dr. Goodfellow is asked to give a medical synopsis of the event for the coroner's jury and writes, "We, the jury, find that John Heath came to his death from emphysema of the lungs, a disease very common at high altitudes. In this case the disease was superinduced by strangulation, self inflicted or otherwise".		
1884, February 24	Diarist George Parsons is the first person to be confirmed in St. Paul's Episcopal church in Tombstone. Bishop Dunlop officiates.		
1884, March 6		The city of Sheridan, Wyoming in incorporated.	
1884, March 20		The city of Laramie, Wyoming is incorporated.	
1884, March 27			The first long distance telephone call is made between Boston and New York City.
1884, March 28	Convicted of murder in the Bisbee Massacre, the remaining 4 bandits are hung simultaneously in Tombstone.		
1884, April 16		Appearing with the Sells Brothers Circus, Annie Oakley is billed for the first time as a markswoman.	
1884, June 2		Lillie Langtry again plays the Cheyenne Opera House.	
1884, July 13		Elizabeth Bonduel Lily Tabor, first child to Horace and "Baby Doe" Tabor is born.	
1884, July 21		"Mysterious" Dave Mather shoots Tom Nixon dead in Dodge City.	
1884, August 5			The cornerstone is laid for the Statue Of Liberty pedestal.

Date	Tombstone Events	Other Old West Events	Events Elsewhere
1884, August 19	Doc Holliday is not doing well in Colorado as his health continues to deteriorate. He has a shooting affray with Billy Allen at Leadville, Colorado over a $5 loan. Holliday will be arrested, then acquitted on the grounds of self-defense.		
1884, August 26			The linotype machine, used to set type, is patented by Ottmar Merganthaler. It is first used by the New York Tribune.
1884, September 11		The Society Of Montana Pioneers is established.	
1884, October 13			Greenwich, England established as universal time meridian of longitude.
1884, November		Wells Fargo reports that between November 1870 and November 1884 there have been over 313 stage robberies and 34 attempted robberies. That's an average of 2 robberies or attempted robberies per month making the stage a pretty dangerous conveyance. Additionally, sixteen stage drivers and guards were shot to death. Sixteen robbers were killed in gun battles while robbing the stages and 240 robbers were convicted and imprisoned.	
1884, December 8		The town of Langtry Texas is incorporated, named after actress Lilly Langtry at the behest of western luminary Judge Roy Bean, a great admirer of the actress.	
1884, December 16			The World Industrial and Cotton Centennial Exposition opens in New Orleans. California grown fruit wins prizes that will result in a California real-estate boom during 1885-1887. Former Tombstone mayor John Clum will later cash-in on the real-estate boom during that time.
1884, December 20		Former cattle-baron, John Chisum dies.	
1884, Other events	Through a number of acquisitions and mergers, the Tombstone Epitaph becomes the Record Epitaph.		A ten story building called the Home Life Insurance Building, the world's first "skyscraper" is completed in Chicago. Using the new technology of hanging floors and walls on a steel skeleton, rather than using heavy and cumbersome masonry. The height of a building is now theoretically limitless.

Date	Tombstone Events	Other Old West Events	Events Elsewhere
1885, January 21			Blues musician, "Leadbelly" is born in Louisiana.
1885, January 25			Future author, Laura Ingalls, 18, marries Almanzo Wilder in the Dakota Territory. She will later write, "The Little House On The Prairie".
1885, February	Securing an appointment as Tombstone's Postmaster, John Clum returns to his favorite frontier town to help with it's rejuvenation.		
1885, February 21			The Washington Monument is dedicated in Washington, DC. The project began July 4, 1848.
1885, February 25		Congress passes a law prohibiting the unauthorized fencing of public western lands with barbed wire.	
1885, February 28			The American Telephone and Telegraph company is incorporated.
1885, Marsh 5			Karl Benz of Germany introduces the first internal combustion automobile.
1885, March 7		To stem an epidemic cattle disease, Kansas makes it illegal to drive Texas cattle through Kansas between March 1 and December 1. The days of the cattle drive are numbered.	
1885, March 13	After perpetrating a fair share of fighting and mayhem Doc Holliday is asked to leave Leadville, Colorado.	President Cleveland warns would-be settlers to stay out of Indian Territory. (present-day Oklahoma)	
1885 Easter Sunday			Jeweler Carl Faberge gives Czar Alexander of Russia the first of what is now the world-famous Faberge egg. The Czar gave the egg to his wife, Empress Marie Feodorovna as a gift.
1885, April 3		The Montana Stockgrower's Association is formed.	
1885, April 23		23 inches of snow fall in Denver in 24 hours. Annie Oakley joins Buffalo Bill's Wild West Show. Her husband, Frank Butler now serves as her manager rather than a performing partner. Butler informs Cody that he does not own Oakley; that she is free to perform wherever she wants in-between Cody engagements.	

Date	Tombstone Events	Other Old West Events	Events Elsewhere
1885, May 10		"Mysterious Dave" Mather and his brother, Josiah get into a gunfight over a card game in Ashland, Kansas. Grocer David Barnes is shot dead and two bystanders are wounded. Both Mather brothers are arrested but quickly post bail and head out of town.	
1885, May 17		Geronimo and over 100 Apaches, who had been living peacefully on the San Carlos Reservation since 1883, escape and head for Mexico after authorities prohibit the alcoholic beverage, Tiswin.	
1885, June 19			The Statue Of Liberty, a gift from France, arrives in New York.
1885, July 23			Former President and military leader, Ulysses S. Grant dies at 63.
1885, October		There are only 20,000 bison left in North America. In 1880, an estimated 395,000 roamed the plains.	
1885, November 3		Race riots against Chinese workers break out in Tacoma, Washington.	
1885, November 19		Ned Buntline's "Will Cody, Pony Express Rider or Buffalo Bill's First Trail" begins serialization in the *Banner Weekly*.	
1885, December 31		The west is wracked with a severe winter. Six-foot drifts are reported in Nebraska.	
1885 Other events	Al Schieffelin, brother to Ed Schieffelin, founder of Tombstone, dies. Judge Wells Spicer who presided over the OK Corral inquest commits suicide. (This date is also given as 1887 (Chaffin)) Nellie Cashman re-opens the Russ House Restaurant in Tombstone. Water continues to seep into Tombstone's mines. Huge pumps are brought in and work well for a short time.	The Los Angeles Times reports "…Los Angeles has three good hotels, twenty-seven churches and 350 public telephone subscribers". John B. Stetson organizes the famous hat company that still bears his name.	Future B movie western star Gabby Hayes is born. Garbage disposal becomes a social problem. There is now so much of it, it can no longer be dumped into lakes and rivers and leaving it to rot creates health problems. Furnaces to burn garbage are put into use in many big cities. Mark Twains' "Huckleberry Finn" is banned in Concord, Massachusetts as "trash suitable only for the slums".

Date	Tombstone Events	Other Old West Events	Events Elsewhere
1886, January	Pete Spence, once a nemesis of the Earps (and other in Tombstone) steps onto the "other side" of the law becoming a Deputy Sheriff in Georgetown, New Mexico.	The mid-west is caught in the grips of an extremely harsh winter. It will come to be known as "The Great Die-Up". The Dodge City Globe reports cattle seen standing on their feet frozen to death. Other reports say that cattle are seen walking with their tail to the wind trying to escape the onslaught until they freeze to death in their tracks.	
1886, February		Cattlemen report losing up to 40% of their herds due to bitter cold weather.	
1886, February 6	Dr Matthews, prominent Tombstone physician dies leaving his practice to Dr. Goodfellow.		
1886, February 7		Race riots against Chinese workers break out in Seattle. Federal troops are required to restore order.	
1886, February 8		Buffalo Bill Cody appears at the Grand Opera House in Topeka, Kansas.	
1886, February 14			The first shipment of California oranges heads east.
1886, March 13		Bat Masterson closes the saloons in Dodge City.	
1886, March 22		Electric lights burn for the first time in Abilene, Kansas. The local newspaper ponders the question of their value.	
1886, April 9		One can now travel from Kansas to California via rail for $12, first class, $7 second class.	
1886, April 15			The San Diego Street Car Company is formed.
1886, April 24	Accompanying General Crook on his quest to for renegade Indian, Geronimo, Tombstone photographer C.S. Fly takes some rare photographs of the Apache Chief just prior to his capture. They are run in the April 24 issue of Harper's Weekly.		
1886, May		Competition amongst railroads drives the price of a ticket from Kansas City to Los Angeles down to $1. California is flooded with emigrants.	
1886, May 12	A fire in Tombstone levels the Grand Central Pump House (pumping water from the mines) causing the mines to fill with water. This is a devastating blow from which the mining operations will never fully recover.		

Date	Tombstone Events	Other Old West Events	Events Elsewhere
1886, June	Doc Holliday is interviewed by a reporter for the *New York Sun*. When asked if he really killed 30 men, Doc replies, "I claim to have been a benefactor to the country!".		
1886, July	Virgil Earp establishes a detective agency in Colton. He gives as reference… "any prominent citizen of Kansas, New Mexico, Arizona or California".		
1886, July 16		Edward Zane Carroll Judson, better known as Ned Buntline, father of the dime novel and the man who started the legend of Buffalo Bill dies in New York.	
1886, July 30	The Silver City *Enterprise* calls Pete Spence "…one of the best peace officers in the west". (See entry for August 6, 1886)		
1886, August 6	The same Pete Spence who was lauded only a week prior for his exploits as a peace officer is arrested for the beating death of Rodney O' Hara, a suspect in his custody. This marked the end of Spence's law enforcement career.	Wyoming's first county fair is held in Johnson County. The *Topeka Daily Capital* notes the proliferation of fairs in the state with 44 planned for the coming year.	
1886, August 14		Prentiss Ingraham's "Buffalo Bill's Swoop, or The King Of the Mines" begins serialization in *Beadle's Dime Library*.	
1886, August 31		Gordon Lillie and Mary Manning are wed. Gordon is better known as "Pawnee Bill" and competes with Buffalo Bill Cody's Wild West Show.	
1886, September 4		Geronimo, the last of the Indian Chiefs gives up to veteran Indian hunter General Nelson Miles. He is shipped off to a reservation in Florida.	
1886, September 15		The first Wyoming Territorial Fair is held in Cheyenne.	
1886, September 27		P.T. Barnum's "Greatest Show On Earth" plays in Topeka, Kansas to 20,000 people.	
1886, October 16		Electric lights are turned on for the first time in Miles City, Montana.	
1886, October 28			The Statue Of Liberty is dedicated.
1886, November 13		Killing blizzards begin in the Plains states providing the worst winter on record. Hundreds of thousands of cattle starve or are frozen to death. It marked the end of open cattle raising since cattlemen now found it necessary to tend their herds in winter to stave off another large-scale massacre.	

Date	Tombstone Events	Other Old West Events	Events Elsewhere
1886, December	Former Clum associate and partner in the original Tombstone Epitaph, Charles Reppy, returns to Tombstone and takes control of what was then The Record-Epitaph. The "Record" is dropped from the name.	In one week, the temperature in Glendive, Montana goes from 50 degrees to minus 35 degrees, an 85-degree drop!	
1886, Other Events	John Clum leaves Tombstone to open an insurance and real-estate office in San Bernardino, CA. The firm of Clum & O'Conner is born. While still operating the Russ House Restaurant in Tombstone, Nellie Cashman opens the Delmonico Hotel in Nogales, A.T. Wyatt and Sadie visit Virgil and Allie in San Diego and decide to stay. Here they run into Bat Masterson, US Marshal.	In Topeka, Kansas, butter costs 20 cents per pound, eggs are 20 cents a dozen, sugar costs $1 for 14 pounds and coffee is 8 pounds for a $1. J.B. "Print" Olive is shot in the head by cowboy Joe Sparrow over a $10 debt. The number of bison in the American West drops to about 1,000.	The Westinghouse Electric Company is established. Steam sterilization of surgical instruments is introduced.
1887, January	Cochise County Sheriff "Texas" John Slaughter kills bandit-murderer Geronimo Baltierrez near Fairbank, A.T., about 8 miles from Tombstone. Slaughter was known to shoot first, and ask questions later but proved very effective as a rancher and peace officer. Although short of stature, men feared him.	Leavenworth, Kansas has 200 saloons.	Kansan Thomas W. Stevens returns to San Francisco after bicycling around the world. He has been gone since April, 1884.
1887, January 1		The Prescott and Arizona Railroad is completed with the driving of another golden spike. Commodore Perry Owens assumes the office of Sheriff of Apache County in Holbrook, Arizona.	
1887, January 5			John L. Sullivan boxes an exhibition match in Topeka, Kansas.
1887, January 20			Pearl Harbor is leased by the US as a naval station.

Date	Tombstone Events	Other Old West Events	Events Elsewhere
1887, February		This is the second harsh winter in a row. San Francisco is hit with a storm that leaves several inches of snow and reportedly, 60% of Montana's cattle have frozen to death. Boston Corbett, the man who shot John Wilkes Booth, recently named doorkeeper for the U.S. House Of Representatives is dismissed for threatening to shoot several people. He will be declared insane and institutionalized. Leavenworth, Kansas, a city of about 24,000 people has 200 saloons.	
1887, March 4		Tempers flare as sheep and cattle industry clash on the plains. One can ride on the Southern-Pacific Railroad, one-way between Missouri and California for $12. Competition will eventually drive the price down to $1.	William Randolph Hearst, recently expelled from Harvard, takes over as publisher of the *San Francisco Examiner*. He is 24 years old.
1887, March 18			Edwin Booth, brother of assassin John Wilkes Booth appears in *Hamlet* in Cheyenne, Wyoming.
1887, April 4		Susanna Salter is elected as America's first female mayor in Argonia, Kansas.	
1887, May	Doc Holliday checks into the Glenwood Sanitarium in Glenwood Springs, Colorado seeking relief from the coughing and choking that he lives with on a daily basis. He is 35 years old, having survived his malady for 14 years. Most consumptives do not live this long.		
1887, May 1		Gunfighter Clay Allison meets an unceremonious death near Pecos. Texas as he is tossed from a wagon that runs over him.	
1887, May 3	An earthquake, originating in northern Mexico rocks southern Arizona. The trickle of ground water into Tombstone's mines becomes a flood. Dr Goodfellow and C.S. Fly visit the hardest hit areas in late May, the doctor to treat the victims and Fly to record the event on film.		

Date	Tombstone Events	Other Old West Events	Events Elsewhere
1887, May 20			The bicycle is becoming more popular. The 8th annual convention of the American Wheelmen is held in St. Louis.
1887, June 1	Joseph Isaac "Ike" Clanton is killed by deputy sheriff J.V. Brighton near Globe, A.T. during a robbery attempt.		
1887, June 20		Buffalo Bill's Wild West Show performs before Queen Victoria in London, England.	
1887, July 3		The Maricopa and Phoenix Railroad opens in Phoenix, A.T.	
1887, July 13	The *Tombstone Epitaph* reports complaints from merchants on Allen Street that the street is littered with so many empty beer barrels that it makes shopping difficult.		
1887, July 23		The largest gold nugget ever found in Colorado is discovered at the Gold-Flake mine. It weighs a whopping 156 ounces. It will later be displayed at the Chicago World's Fair.	
1887, July 27	Virgil Earp is elected the first Marshal of Colton, California. His salary is $75 per month. His father, Nicholas Earp is elected Justice Of The Peace.		
1887, July 31	Due to Tombstone's decline, The Epitaph becomes weekly newspaper once again. Hoping for Tombstone's rejuvenation, The Epitaph would go back and forth between daily and weekly several more times in the coming years.		
1887, August 9		Harry Longabaugh, later known as the Sundance Kid, is convicted of grand larceny in Sundance, Colorado.	
1887, August 19		The last Indian and US Army battle held in Colorado is fought.	
1887, September 2		Near Holbrook, A.T., Andy Blevins attacks a group of sheepherders killing John Tewksbury and William Jacobs.	

74

Date	Tombstone Events	Other Old West Events	Events Elsewhere
1887, September 3	May and Buckskin Frank Leslie are divorced. May charged that Frank physically abused her. In her testimony, May noted that Frank would stand her against a wall and fire his .45's at her forming a silhouette around her body. Thus, May became known as the "Silhouette Girl".		
1887, September 4		Holbrook Sheriff C.P. Owens goes to the Blevins home to arrest Andy Blevins for the shooting of Tewksbury and Jacobs. A melee breaks out and Owens shoots four Blevins family members dead.	
1887, September 5			Labor Day becomes a legal holiday in Oregon. Soon, many other states will observe this end-of-summer holiday.
1887, November 8	Doc Holliday dies in Glenwood Springs, Colorado where he had been bathing in the sulpher springs to relieve his tuberculosis. Ironically, the treatment he thought would bring him at least relief if not longer life, actually hastened his death.		
1887, November 27		U.S. Marshal Frank Dalton is killed in the line of duty. Frank was the "only good Dalton", his brothers all choosing outlawry and paying high prices fro their choices.	
1887, December 22		The Butte Miners band organizes in Butte, Montana.	
1887, Other events	Charles Davidson builds a house in Colton, California at 528 "H" Street at a cost of $400. It is sold to Sam B. Fox in 1888 and then from Fox to F.W. Walin later that year. On November 7, 1888 Virgil Earp purchased the house for $400. Former Cochise County Sheriff Johnny Behan begins his term as Superintendent of Yuma Territorial prison. With the mines failing and the local economy in a slump, George W. Parson leaves Tombstone for Los Angeles.	With the arrival of thousands of immigrants to California thanks to cheap transportation, land prices in Los Angeles soar. Prices go from $100 to $1,500 per acre. This trend will soon peak. (See entry for Autumn, 1888.) Sharpshooter Annie Oakley leaves Buffalo Bill's Wild West Show to tour with a similar shown managed by Pawnee Bill.	Mail is now delivered free to all communities over 10,000. Golf is officially established in the US with the founding of the Foxburg Golf Club in Foxburg, PA. The US-Hawaii Treaty is renewed and ratified with an amendment giving the US exclusive rights to establish a naval base at Pearl Harbor.
1888, January			The National Geographic Society forms in Washington, DC.

Date	Tombstone Events	Other Old West Events	Events Elsewhere
1888, January 21		Stage-robber Charles Boles, aka Black Bart is released from prison after serving 4 of his 6 year term. He is 59 years old.	
1888, February		Now having one of Buffalo Bill's former star attractions, Annie Oakley, Pawnee Bill plans to compete head-to-head with his idol.	
1888, March 4			Football coach Knute Rockne is born.
1888, March 14			A huge blizzard blankets the east coast. 200 die in New York City alone.
1888, March 24		Ella Watson who will later be known as Cattle Annie stakes a claim for property in Wyoming. She will open a log-cabin bordello and begin dabbling in stolen cattle.	
1888, April		Refrigerated railroad cars begin shipping California-grown produce to the east coast.	
1888, April 9	Virgil Earp is re-elected as the Marshal of Colton, California.		
1888, April 13			Actor Edwin Booth, brother to the more infamous John Wilkes Booth, performs in the Shakespearean play, *Othello*, in Topeka, Kansas.
1888, June 1		Two men sit in a Florence, A.T. saloon arguing over politics. One thing leads to another, guns are drawn, shots are fired, and the two men lay dead. "Politics" is given as the cause of death.	
1888, June 7	Cochise County Sheriff John Slaughter and deputy Burt Alvord chase Mexican bandits into the Whetstone Mountains just outside of Tombstone. As is his custom, Slaughter will sneak up on the bandits at dawn, order them to surrender, and immediately shoot them dead.		
1888, June 24		Kingman, A. T. is destroyed by fire.	
1888, July 4	Mattie Blaylock Earp, Wyatt's second wife is found dead, at Pinal A.T., apparently of a drug overdose.		
1888, October 1			Congress forbids the return to the United States of any Chinese who have left the country.
1888, October 17			First issue of National Geographic appears.

Date	Tombstone Events	Other Old West Events	Events Elsewhere
1888, October 23		The Jerome stage is robbed near Jerome, A.T. The hapless bandits net about $30.	
1888, November 7	Virgil Earp buys a house at 528 H Street in Colton, CA for $400.		
1888, November 22		Bandits rob a stage near Florence, A.T. taking only $26 from the passengers and taking the Wells-Fargo box.	
1888, November 28	The Post Office at Contention City closes and the town is abandoned.		
1888, Autumn	To help rejuvenate a failing California real-estate market, San Bernardino realtor John Clum promotes California citrus fruit to the east coast. He fails to bring real estate investors to southern California but inadvertently gives a major boost to the citrus fruit industry.		
1888, Other Events	Josephine Marcus and Wyatt Earp are wed in Parker, A.T.	Theodore Roosevelt publishes *Ranch Life and the Hunting Trails*. Frederick Remington illustrates the book.	William S. Burroughs develops the first successful adding machine. George Eastman perfects the Kodak hand camera allowing the average person to easily shoot photographs. The camera holds enough film for 100 photos. Once the film is exposed, the owner returns the camera to Kodak. The photographs are returned with the camera re-loaded with enough film for an additional 100 pictures.
1889, January 1		An eclipse of the sun, "predicted" (with the aid of an almanac) by Paiute Indian Wovoka, marks the start of the "Ghost Dance" religion which believes that departed ancestors would rise from the dead and reclaim land taken by the white man.	New York state replaces death by hanging with the electric chair as the preferred method of capital punishment.
1889, January 29		Arizona's legislature votes to move the territorial capital from Prescott to Phoenix.	

Date	Tombstone Events	Other Old West Events	Events Elsewhere
1889, February	In Tombstone, Cochise County Deputy Sheriff Burt Alvord sits in a saloon with two men, Fuller and Fortino. An argument develops and Fuller grabs Alvord's gun, shooting Fortino dead. Alvord is reprimanded by his boss, Cochise County Sheriff John Slaughter for even associating with the likes of those men.		
1889, February 3		Belle Starr is ambushed and murdered near Eufalfa, Indian Territory, felled by a shotgun blast to her back. Her attacker is never found.	
1889, February 4		Harry Longabaugh is released from the Crook County jail and assumes the alias "Sundance Kid".	
1889, February 22			Washington, Montana and North and South Dakota are admitted into the Union. An article in a Topeka, Kansas newspaper reports that cigarettes are killing off "a good many promising boys".
1889, February 25			Blacks in Kansas push to end discrimination in public schools.
1889, March 9	Virgil Earp resigns his post as City Marshal of Colton, CA.		
1889, March 23		President Benjamin Harrison announces the pending opening of the former Indian Territory for settlement.	
1889, April 12		Buffalo Bill's Wild West Show departs for France. Rejoining him, after spending a year with Pawnee Bill, is Annie Oakley.	
1889 April 22		At exactly noon, the Oklahoma land rush is on.	
1889, April 29		Buffalo Bill's Wild West Show opens in Paris.	
1889, May			Band leader Duke Ellington is born .
1889, June		Future President Teddy Roosevelt publishes, "The Winning Of The West" covering a period from Daniel Boone to present.	
1889 June 27		A Telluride bank is reportedly robbed by Butch Cassidy and the Sundance Kid.	

78

Date	Tombstone Events	Other Old West Events	Events Elsewhere
1889, July10	In Tombstone, Buckskin Frank Leslie shoots his girlfriend, Molly Williams in a drunken rage over her affair with ranch-hand Jim Neal. He tries to shoot Neal who escapes and informs authorities. Frank is arrested.		
1889, July 20		Ella Watson, aka "Cattle Kate" and her lover, Jim Averill are hanged by vigilantes for stealing cattle. Cattle Kate was reportedly the only woman ever hanged for cattle rustling.	
1889, July 23			Boxers John L. Sullivan and Jake Kilrain fight for 75 rounds before Sullivan is victorious.
1889, July 24		Butch Cassidy and friends rob the San Miguel Valley Bank in Telluride, CO.	
1889, August	Dr. Goodfellow is fined $25 in Justice Easton's court for carrying a concealed weapon (a knife) in connection with his assault on Frank White on Allen St in Tombstone.		
1889, September 16		Robert Younger dies at 35 years of age of "consumption" in the Stillwater Penitentiary. He was serving a life sentence for his part in the Northfield, Minnesota bank robbery in 1876.	
1889, October 14		A Wyoming grand jury fails to indict anyone for the lynching of Cattle Kate and Jim Averill citing lack of evidence.	
1889, November 12			Future cowboy star Buck Jones is born.
1889, November 17			The Union Pacific Railroad begins service between Chicago and Portland, OR.
1889, November 23			The first juke box is installed in San Francisco
1889, December 6			Former president of the Confederacy, Jefferson Davis dies in New Orleans.
1889, December 10	Buckskin Frank Leslie is found guilty in the shooting death of his former girlfriend, Molly Williams. And sentenced to 25 years of hard labor at the Yuma Territorial Prison. He is Inmate 632. He will serve less than 8 years and is thought to have headed for the Alaska gold fields.		

Date	Tombstone Events	Other Old West Events	Events Elsewhere
1889, Other events	One-time owner of the Oriental Saloon and one of Tombstone's leading citizen's during it's hay-day, Milt Joyce, dies. He is only 42. Former Tombstoner, Nellie Cashman, after a failed bid to marry a prosperous miner, travels to several other mining boomtowns looking for the next big strike. She goes to Bodie, California, Couer d'Alene, Idaho, Wyoming and Montana.		Bicycling becomes popular with the advent of the safety bicycle. William Kennedy Laurie Dickson makes "Fred Ott's Sneeze" the first celluloid film. There are now less then 1100 buffalo alive in the US.
1890, January 25			26year old Nellie Bly, one of the earliest newspaper reporters completes a globe circling trip in the then astounding time of 72 days, 6 hours and 11 minutes.
1890, March 3		Buffalo Bill's Wild West Show plays in Rome, Italy.	
1890, April 9	Former U.S. Marshal Crawley Dake dies in Prescott, A.T.		
1890, May			Future author Jack London drops out of school at 14 to work odd jobs to help his financially strapped family.
1890, May 25		An electric street railway is established in Helena, Montana.	
1890, June 16			Future funny-man Stan Laurel is born.
1890, July 1		North Dakota observes prohibition.	The cornerstone for the Colorado statehouse is laid. The building, costing $2,800,000 will be completed in 1894.
1890, July 23		Buffalo Bill's Wild West Show opens in Berlin, Germany. Meanwhile in the US, dime novels about the exploits of Buffalo Bill and Wild Bill Hickok fuel the public's passion of the old-west culture.	
1890, September 25			Giving in to increasing government pressure, the Mormon Church denounces plural marriages.
1890, October 1			Yosemite National Park is dedicated.
1890, October 14			Future military leader and President, Dwight David Eisenhower is born in Denison, Texas.
1890, October 16		Indians dancing the Ghost Dance are scaring military leaders at the Standing Rock and Pine Ridge reservations in South Dakota.	

Date	Tombstone Events	Other Old West Events	Events Elsewhere
1890, October 21	Virgil Earp applies and gets a military pension. It is $12 per month.		
1890, November			The May Company in Denver advertises overcoats for $15 and derbies for $1.98.
1890, November 29			First Army-Navy football game -Navy 24, Army 0.
1890, December		Indians on South Dakota reservations continue to scare the military with their Ghost Dance. Fearing a total Indian uprising, area residents arm themselves with government-afforded weaponry.	
1890, December 15		Sitting Bull is arrested for his part in the Ghost Dance at a nearby reservation. During his apprehension by Indian Police, he struggles and is shot dead. His horse, given to him by Buffalo Bill and trained to prance at the sound of gunfire begins to prance about. The Indians interpret this as a Ghost Dance.	
1890, December 29		Fearing for their lives seeing Indians dance themselves into frenzy, the military tries to disarm South Dakota reservation Indians. A fight breaks out and soldiers are ordered to shoot Indians. As many as 150 may have died that day although no accurate count has ever been established. It will become known as the Massacre At Wounded Knee.	
1890, Other Events		The US population is 62,979,766, double what it was before the Civil War. With 11,000,000 settlers settled west of the Mississippi, the census bureau declares the frontier closed. The rural population is 84% The population of Los Angeles is 50,000. Denver has grown from 35,000 in 1880 to over 106,000 in 1890.	A labor strike is averted at Adolph Coors brewery in Colorado. After years of Indian slaughter by the US military and the deaths of many Indians due to disease introduced by white Europeans, the Indian population in California has dropped from 100,000 to 18,000.
1891, January 6		Sioux Indians attack a wagon train near the site of the Wounded Knee massacre. It will be the last recorded Sioux attack on white settlers.	
1891, April 10			Future movie cowboy Tim McCoy is born.
1891, May 17		Relics from the ill-fated Donner party of 1846-47 are unearthed near Truckee, California.	

81

Date	Tombstone Events	Other Old West Events	Events Elsewhere
1891, July	Virgil Earp sells his home at 528 H Street in Colton for $1250 making a 320% profit on the real estate in only 3 years.	Winfield Stratton strikes silver near Cripple Creek, Colorado. A carpenter by trade, Stratton works the diggings himself making thousands of dollars, more so than if he had been banging nails. Eight years later he will sell his interest in the mine to European investors for $10M.	
1891, August 16	Suffering from consumption since 1876, Katherine, Mrs George Goodfellow dies in Oakland, CA.		
1891, Autumn		Western luminary Tom Horn sets a new record for steer roping at the Arizona Territorial Fair in Phoenix.	
1891, October 4	Dr. George Goodfellow accepts a job as company doctor for the Southern Pacific Railroad moving to Tucson thus ending his Tombstone period.		
1891, October 25	A large send-off party is held in the Mining Exchange Building on Fremont St in Tombstone for Dr. George Goodfellow. Among those speaking at the gala event is C.S. Fly. Master of ceremonies is famed Tombstone Attorney Marcus Smith.		
1891, November	Following the precedent of Tucson and many other southwestern cities, Tombstone begins promoting itself as "health haven" – a place where consumptives and others with chronic diseases could regain their health. The Cochise County Hospital begins operating as the "Tombstone Sanitarium".		
1891, Other Events		Artists Charles M. Russell sketches the last Ghost Dances at the Pine Ridge Indian Reservation.	Whitcomb Judson patents the zipper. James Naismith of Springfield, MA invents the game of basketball. The first Boston Marathon is run. The first "Del Monte" canned goods are produced in California.
1892, January 20			The first basketball game is played in Springfield, MA.
1892, March 1			Thomas Edison introduces moving pictures at his studio in West Orange, NJ.

82

Date	Tombstone Events	Other Old West Events	Events Elsewhere
1892, March 18	Pete Spence is arrested for the first of what would be 5 killings in what is purported to be "Pete's Mexican Vendetta", all his victims being Mexicans. This would lead to his eventual incarceration in the Yuma Territorial Prison.		
1892, April 8		Butch Cassidy is arrested for horse theft in Wyoming.	
1892, June 8		Bob Ford murderer of Jesse James is himself murdered by glory-seeker Edward O' Kelly.	
1892, July 22	Milton B. Clapp, member of Tombstone's Citizen's Safety Committee (Vigilante group) and founding incorporator of the Tombstone Epitaph commits suicide in Los Angeles, CA.		
1892, July 23		Congress bans liquor sales to all Indians living on reservations.	
1892, August 6			Future movie cowboy Hoot Gibson is born.
1892, October 12			Buildings are dedicated in a ceremony at the site of what will soon be the 1893 World's Columbian Exposition in Chicago.
1892, October 15		The Dalton Gang tries unsuccessfully to brazenly rob two banks at once in Coffeyville, Kansas. Their false whiskers disguises don't fool anyone and they are cut down in a hail of lead.	
1892, Other Events		The town of Cripple Creek, Colorado is incorporated. It is one of the richest mining districts in Colorado. In 1892, $500,000 worth of gold was dug up. At its peak in 1900, $18 million worth of gold was taken from the ground around Cripple Creek. As late as 1917 it was still being mined and produced $17 million dollars that year.	The first electric and first gasoline powered automobiles are seen in the US.
1893, May 1			The 1893 World's Columbian Exposition opens in Chicago. Over the next 6 months approximately 27.5 million people will visit the Exposition, also called the 1893 World's fair. President Grover Cleveland officiated the opening ceremonies.
1893, May 5			The stock market collapses taking with it 600 banks and over 15,000 businesses.

Date	Tombstone Events	Other Old West Events	Events Elsewhere
1893, June 1	Newly appointed Arizona Territory Governor L.C. Hughs establishes the office of "Territorial Quarantine and Health Officer" appointing now Tucson resident Dr. George Goodfellow to the post. The area is expecting a cholera epidemic.		
1893, June 10	Pete Spence is sentenced to five years in the Yuma Territorial prison for the charge of "aggravated assault" on one Ramon Estella.		
1893, July		In an address to the American Historical Association during the 1893 World's Columbian Exhibition in Chicago, a 32 year old Doctor of History, Frederick Jackson Turner, declares the western frontier closed echoing the findings of the US Census Bureau of 1890.	
1893, September 16		The Cherokee Strip, a plot of land 165 miles long by 85 miles wide in Oklahoma is opened to settlers.	
1893, October 9			Over 700,000 people, a fair record, visit the 1893 World's Columbian Exhibition on "Chicago Day".
1893, October 14	With the passing of Virginia Ann Earp (Wyatt's mother) Nicholas Porter Earp marries his third wife, Annie Alexander in San Bernardino. He is 80; she is 51.		
1893, October 26			The 1893 World's Columbian Exposition closes in Chicago. Future historians will dub this the most significant fair, and one of the more significant events of the 19th century!
1893, November 1		The Sherman Silver Purchase Act is repealed and the US returns to the gold standard. The price of silver drops like a rock to 77 cents an ounce. Banks close all over the US. In Colorado the Bureau Of Labor Statistics reveal 377 business failures, 435 mines closed, and 45,000 people out of work. Financier Horace Tabor finds himself over $2m in debt overnight.	

Date	Tombstone Events	Other Old West Events	Events Elsewhere
1893, November 4	Virgil and Allie Earp leave Colton for the California boomtown of Vanderbilt where he builds a 2 story building called Earp's hall.		
1893, Other events		Noted period thespian and brother of the man who shot Abraham Lincoln. Edwin Booth dies.	Attempts to have the US change over the metric system fail.
		Oil is struck while drilling for water in Corsican, Texas.	Katherine Lee Bates authors the words to "America The Beautiful".
1894, January	Photographer C.S. Fly is elected Cochise County Sheriff. He won, "not because he had so many friends but because he had so few enemies". He would serve one term.		The Janesville Weekly Gazette in Wisconsin advertises a men's sack suit for $7. Info courtesy of Joan Severa, author, Dressed For The Photographer – Ordinary Americans and Fashion 1840-1900
1894, February 17		Texas governor Jim Hogg pardons outlaw John Wesley Hardin, after spending 16 years in prison for the 1874 murder of a Texas Sheriff.	
1894, May 5		Porter Perrin Wheaton, a civil and mining engineer begins a 2328 mile trek around southern California collecting data which would be used to produce the first surveyor's map of San Diego county. To gather the data he pushes a wheelbarrow containing an odometer, clinometer and compass. He completes his journey December 29, 1894.	
1894, Spring	Hundreds of Tombstoners leave town for the new mining strike in what will become the town of Pearce, about 20 miles east and north of Tombstone. Many will return no richer. Many will work for the Pearce family.		
1894, July 15		Butch Cassidy is convicted of horse stealing and enters a prison in Wyoming.	
1894, September	Nellie Cashman opens a restaurant and boarding house in Jerome, A.T., northeast of Prescott.		

Date	Tombstone Events	Other Old West Events	Events Elsewhere
1894, November Thanksgiving Day	After serving only 15 months of a five year sentence for aggravated assault, Pete Spence is released from Yuma Prison on a pardon from Governor L. C. Hughs. Spence was noted to be an ideal prisoner. Further, sworn affidavits by eye witnesses noted that Spence had been provoked, certain parties making public threats against his life forcing Spence to act in his own defense.		
1894, December 27	Virgil & Allie Earp head for Cripple Creek, Colorado where they join Wyatt.		
1894, Other events			Actor Walter Brennan is born.
			A fire at the World's Columbian Exposition in Chicago nearly destroys all buildings.
			The Sunday comics first appear.
			The first commercial chili-powder is marketed by German-American William Gebhardt. Fittingly, it is in Texas.
1895, January 8			Future film director John Ford is born.
1895, June 5			Future actor, best known for his portrayal of Hopalong Cassidy, William Boyd is born.
1895, July	Dr. George Goodfellow resigns his post as Chief Surgeon with the Southern Pacific Railroad to resume private practice.	Alcatraz Island is designated a military jail.	
1895, July 27			Future movie cowboy, Ken Maynard is born.
1895, August 19		Outlaw John Wesley Hardin is shot and killed by John Selman at the Acme Saloon in El Paso, TX.	
1895, October	Virgil and Allie arrive in Prescott, A.T. where Virgil returns to mining.

Nellie Cashman opens yet another restaurant in Globe, A.T. | | |

Date	Tombstone Events	Other Old West Events	Events Elsewhere
1895, Other events		Less than 1000 bison roam the west.	Future western matinee star Ken Maynard is born. Sears-Roebuck establishes a mail-order business. H.G. Wells publishes "The Time Machine".
1896, January 15		Lawman Bill Tilghman captures outlaw Bill Doolin at a bath house in Eureka Springs, Arkansas.	
1896, January 19		Butch Cassidy is released from the Wyoming State Prison at Laramie.	
1896, January 20			Actor and comedian George Burns is born.
1896, March 31			The first zipper is patented.
1896, Summer		Gold is discovered in Canada's Klondike area near Alaska starting yet another gold-rush. Joseph Ladue (formerly Ledoux) erects a sawmill, at the confluence of the Klondike and Yukon rivers and founds the gold rush town of Dawson. By providing building materials, and through careful land speculation, Ladue became one of a handful of gold rush millionaires.	
1896, August 25		A posse led by lawman Heck Thomas guns down Oklahoma outlaw Bill Doolin. A shot-gun blast fills Doolin with 21 holes.	
1896, September 15			In a staged "accident" in Texas, two railroad engines running at almost 100 miles per hour are smashed together. The flying debris injures two of the 5,000 spectators.
1896, November 17	At the request of Dr. George Goodfellow, Tombstone Attorney Marcus Smith, Judge J.J. Hawkins, and others, Arizona Governor Benjamin J. Franklin pardons Buckskin Frank Leslie who is serving time in Yuma Territorial Prison.		

Date	Tombstone Events	Other Old West Events	Events Elsewhere
1896, December 2	Wyatt referees a boxing match between Ruby Bob Fitzsimmons and Tom Sharkey. Wyatt decides in Sharkey's favor after Fitzsimmons lands a "foul" punch. Sharkey is carried from the ring and the controversy continues for weeks afterwards.		
1896, Other Events	Wyatt and Josie Earp take up living in San Francisco. Wyatt has a stable of race horses.	The Tabor Grand Opera House and Tabor Block are sold to help Horace Tabor settle a legal dispute.	First moving picture on a public screen is seen in New York City.
1897, February 6		A Texas posse captures the last of the Dalton Gang.	
1897, March 17			Bob Fitzsimmons defeats Gentleman Jim Corbett for the heavyweight boxing title in Carson City, Nevada.
1897, May 23	Tombstone founder Ed Schieffelin dies penniless and is buried with his pick, shovel, and canteen three miles from Tombstone on the site of his first camp.		
1897, June 12		The last legal hanging in South Dakota took the life of Isadore Cavanaugh convicted of killing a woman with a meat cleaver.	
1897, July 1	"Justice Jim" Burnett is killed by William C. Green in what is described as the second shoot-out at the OK Corral. Nellie Cashman opens the Hotel Cashman in Yuma, A.T.		
1897, August 23		Realizing the western frontier is practically gone now, the first Frontier Days celebration is held in Cheyenne, Wyoming.	
1897, Other Events	Former Tombstone luminary Buckskin Frank Leslie heads to the Klondike in search of gold.	Gold prospectors begin to head for the Klondike region of Canada's Yukon Territory. The first Cheyenne frontier Days is held in Cheyenne, WY.	The first practical subway is established in Boston. A 14 round boxing match between Jim Corbett and Bob Fitzsimmons is the first match captured by a moving picture camera.
1898, February 15			The battleship "USS Maine" blows up and sinks in Havana Harbor in Cuba thus starting the Spanish-American War.

Date	Tombstone Events	Other Old West Events	Events Elsewhere
1898, March 29	Nancy Jane Adams Earp, wife of Newton Jasper Earp, dies.		The Spanish-American War begins.
1898, April 22	Nellie Cashman arrives in Dawson, AK.		
1898, May 23	The Arizona Daily Citizen reports that Dr. George Goodfellow is in Tucson preparing to leave for Tampa, Florida, having been appointed to serve on General Shafter's staff in the Spanish-American War.		
1898, July 1		Former lawman and mayor of Prescott, A.T., Buckey O' Neill is killed in action in Cuba.	
		Future president Teddy Roosevelt leads Rough Riders up Cuba's Kettle Hill during the Spanish-American War.	
1898, Summer	In the wake of the Klondike gold strike, John Clum is appointed Postmaster for Alaska and will establish post offices in each small town he encounters. He first arrives in Dawson where he runs into former Tombstoner, Nellie Cashman who is again operating a restaurant.	Actress and socialite Lillie Langtry's personal fortune is estimated at over two million dollars. She is 46 years old.	
		Con-man Soapy Smith is shot dead in Skagway, Alaska. He was known for selling bars of soap at trumped-up prices with the promise that customers may find currency up to $100 rolled up in the soap's package.	
		Future aviatrix, Amerlia Earhart is born.	
1898, Other events	Wyatt and Josie Earp head for Alaska.	The Klondike Gold Rush moves into high gear.	Future star of many western movies, Randolph Scott is born.
	Earp friend Sherman McMasters dies in the Philippines. (He may have also been known as Henry McMaster (Chaffin))	Having lost all his money in the silver panic of 1893, noted Denver financier Horace Tabor is working 10-hour days in a smelter. He is 67 years old. His friends have him appointed the postmaster of Denver.	The *Holland*, the first modern submarine is launched.
		Cripple Creek Bar Room, the first western and one of the first movies, is produced. Though lacking a plot, and shot in New Jersey, it is popular due to its sheer novelty.	H.G. Wells publishes "The War Of The Worlds".
1899, January	Virgil and Allie Earp travel to Portland, OR where Virgil meets a daughter that he didn't know existed, born to his first wife, Ellen Donahoo.		Scott Joplin, a black man born to freed slaves rides high as the "King Of Ragtime" a popular musical style of the era.
1899, March 6			Aspirin is patented.

Date	Tombstone Events	Other Old West Events	Events Elsewhere
1899, April 10		Former Denver financier Horace Tabor dies.	
1899, May 10			The first automobile delivered in Denver goes to a David Brunton.
1899, Spring	Wyatt and Josie Earp go to Alaska where they meet John Clum, George Parsons and other former Tombstoners.		
1899, June 2		Butch Cassidy, the Sundance Kid and the Wild Bunch rob a train in Wilcox, Wyoming taking $30,000.	
1899, September	Wyatt and C.E. Hoxie open the Dexter Saloon in Nome, AK. (First called Anvil City.) It is one of the first permanent wooden structures. They make money hand-over-fist. Receipts are $1500 to $2000 per day!		
1899, November 29	Milt Joyce, former owner of the Oriental Saloon, and Wyatt's first employer in Tombstone, dies.		
1899, Other Events			President William McKinley is the first president to ride in an automobile. It is a Stanley Steamer.
1900-1910	Throughout the decline of Tombstone, The Epitaph helped kept spirits up maintaining that Tombstone's salvation, and the rise of silver prices was just around the corner.		
1900, January			Representative George H. White of North Carolina, the last African-American elected during the Reconstruction era introduces a bill to Congress to make lynching a federal crime. The bill never gets out of committee. There are 115 recorded lynchings in 1900.
1900, February 16		Prohibitionist Carrie Nation walks into her first saloon in Kansas and destroys a whisky barrel. This will be the first of many.	
1900, April 28	Wyatt Earp and Tom Mulqueen get into an argument at the Peerless Saloon in San Francisco over horse racing. Wyatt gets knocked out.		

Date	Tombstone Events	Other Old West Events	Events Elsewhere
1900, July 6	Warren Earp is shot and killed by Johnny Boyett in the Headquarters Saloon in Wilcox, A.T. Warren allegedly threatened Boyett.		
1900, July 15	The New York Tribune carries a story about Wyatt Earp being shot in the arm at his saloon, the Dexter, in Nome, Alaska. The shot was allegedly fired during an argument with a patron. The report was apparently false. Info courtesy Casey Teffertiller – Wyatt Earp – The Life Behind The Legend		
1900, July 22			Fifty-five American athletes complete their domination of the second modern Olympic games in Paris.
1900, July 27			H.J. Heinz incorporated.
1900, August 30	Wyatt meets with two old Tombstone friends, John Clum and George Parsons, in Nome Alaska. They talk about old times. Parsons notes that Wyatt runs one of the largest saloons in the area and it is well to be known as his friend. Info courtesy Casey Teffertiller – Wyatt Earp – The Life Behind The Legend		
1900, October 5			Outfielder Honus Wagner hits .381 to win his first of eight batting titles.
1900, October 15	A Post Office is established at the new copper mining town of Gleeson, A.T. providing some work for straining Tombstone residents.		
1900, November 8			"Gone With The Wind" author Margaret Mitchell is born.
1900, November 21		Butch Cassidy, the Sundance Kid and others known as "the Wild Bunch" pose for a now famous picture in Fort Worth, TX.	
1900, Other events	Former Tombstone stage-line owner, Sandy Bob Crouch and Former Tombstone judge, William Herring die.

A friend of the Earps, Texas Jack Vermillion drowns. | The population of Los Angeles exceeds 100,000.

The US Census shows Colorado with a 30% increase in population as opposed to a 20% average for the rest of the country.

The sheep population greatly outpaces the cattle population in Wyoming.

Tom Horn kills Matt Rash and Isom Dart. | The first trial flight of the Zeppelin is made in Germany.

New York is the largest city in the US with 3.4 million people.

The average life expectancy for a man is 48. Women get to live a little longer at 51. Wyatt Earp is 52. |

Date	Tombstone Events	Other Old West Events	Events Elsewhere
1901, January 10		Oil is discovered at Spindletop in Beaumont, Texas. This marks the start of a new type of business industrialist, the so-called "oil tycoon" adding to the land barons, cattle barons, mining speculators, and railroad magnates.	
1901, February 1	Former Pima County Sheriff Bob Paul dies.		Actor Clark Gable is born.
1901, March 26			
1901, May 7			Actor Gary Cooper is born.
1901, May 21			Connecticut enacts the first speed limit for vehicles, 12mph.
1901, June 17		Stage robber Bill Miner is released into the 20th century after serving 20 years in San Quentin. The stage coach will continue to be used as a conveyance in many remote corners of the US for several more years. But the world Bill Miner left behind in 1881, is now mostly a memory.	
1901, July 3		Butch Cassidy and the Sundance Kid, along with fellow gang members Harvey Logan, and Camilla Hanks rob a train near Wagner, Montana. This will be the last "Wild Bunch" robbery.	
1901, July 14		After serving the last 25 years of their life behind bars for the ill-fated Northfield, Minnesota bank robbery, Jim and Cole Younger are finally released from Stillwater Penitentiary in Minnesota.	
1901, July 18		Thinking he is shooting rancher Kels Nickell, suspected of rustling cattle, hired shooter Tom Horn kills 14 year-old Willie Nickell, Kel's son.	
1901, August 14	Pete Spence is reported meeting old friends and visiting in Tombstone.		
1901, September 6			President McKinley is shot twice at point-blank range by anarchist Leon Czolgosz at Buffalo, NY.
1901, September 14			President McKinley dies making Theodore Roosevelt President at age 42.
1901, October 12	C.S. Fly dies in Bisbee, AZ and is buried in Tombstone in the city cemetery, not the more-famed boothill.		

Date	Tombstone Events	Other Old West Events	Events Elsewhere
1901, October 29		A train carrying Buffalo Bill's Wild West show wrecks in North Carolina. Star performer, Annie Oakley is injured and will spend several months in the hospital recuperating. (Note: This information is also given as October 28 in Lexington, KY.)	
1901, December 12			Guglielmo Marconi receives the first trans-Atlantic wireless message. He writes, "I now felt for the first time absolutely certain that the day would come when mankind would be able to send messages without wires not only across the Atlantic but between the farthermost ends of the earth".
1901, Other Events			Oil is struck in Texas near Beaumont. J.P. Morgan and Elbert Gary form US Steel, marking the beginning of the end for cattle and railroad barons inasmuch as wealth and power are concerned.
1902, March 4			The American Automobile Association is formed in Chicago.
1902, April 2			The first moving-picture theater opens in Los Angeles. Ironically, "western's" produced in movie studios on the east coast can now be seen on the west coast. A landmark movie, "The Great Train Robbery" featuring actor George Barnes shooting directly into the camera will debut in 1903.
1902, April 14			The J.C. Penney store opens for business in Kemmerer, Wyoming.
1902, April 29			The Senate votes to extend the Chinese Exclusion Act for the second time, barring Chinese immigration into the United States and thus protecting American jobs from cheap Asian labor.
1902, May 28		The first serious western, *The Virginian*, is published. This book is a stark contrast to the "pulp fiction" of its day, the Dime Novel.	
1902, June 19			Bandleader Guy Lombardo is born.

Date	Tombstone Events	Other Old West Events	Events Elsewhere
1902, July 25	Writer Frank Waters is born. He will later author a book about Wyatt Earp which Sadie (Josephine) will try to block saying that it contains only lies and does not portray Wyatt the way she wants him portrayed.		
1902, October 16		Carrie Nation brings her crusade against alcohol to Austin ,Texas and to the campus of the University Of Texas in search of drunken professors.	
1902, October 19		Only out of jail for three months after serving a 25 year sentence, Jim Younger commits suicide. He is 54 years old.	
1902, October 26		Tom Horn is found guilty of killing 14 year old Willie Nickell at Cheyenne, Wyoming.	
1902, November 30		Wild Bunch member Harvey Logan is sentenced to 20 years of hard labor for train robbery.	
1902, Other Events	Wyatt and Sadie (Josephine) Earp return from Alaska with about $80,000. (about $1.6M today)	Calamity Jane, self-proclaimed paramour of Wild Bill Hickok is jailed in Montana for disturbing the peace. The buffalo population in the US begins to rise from an 1895 low of less than 1,000 head.	Olive drab is adopted as the official uniform color of the US Army. The traditional blue proved to be too easily seen by the enemy during the Spanish American war.
1903, January 23			Future cowboy start Randolph Scott is born.
1903, March 16		Judge Roy Bean dies at his beloved saloon, the Jersey Lilly. He is 78 years old.	
1903, May 5	The first train of the El Paso & Southwestern Railroad steams into Tombstone. Ironically, silver prices remain low and Tombstone mines are still full of water.		
1903, July 4		President Roosevelt sends the first round-the-world telegraph message. It takes 12 minutes to circle the globe.	
1903, August 1		Martha Jane Cannary aka Calamity Jane dies at 51 years old and is buried next to Wild Bill Hickok. As a sign of affection for Hickok which was never returned in real life, she has her death date falsified on her tombstone to read August 2, the same death date as Hickok.	
1903, August 9		Tom Horn and another prisoner make an ill-fated attempt at escape from a Cheyenne, Wyoming jail.	

94

Date	Tombstone Events	Other Old West Events	Events Elsewhere
1903, September 23		Going back to his former profession, outlaw Bill Miner and his gang rob a train outside of Portland, Oregon.	
1903, October 16			Future movie cowboy Wild Bill Elliot is born.
1903, November 20		Tom Horn, peace officer and hired killer is executed for the death of Willie Nickell.	
1903, December 17			The Wright brothers fly for the first time at Kitty Hawk, NC.
1903, December 30			A fire in Chicago's Iroquois theatre during a performance by Eddie Foy kills 588 people.
1903, Other events		One of the earliest western movies, "The Great Train Robbery" is seen in public prompting the first movie star, Max Aronson. Although, by this time, the western frontier had been declared officially closed, many "frontiersmen" were still kicking including Bat Masterson, Wyatt Earp, and Geronimo.	Ward Bond is born. Television's "Wagon Train" will be his claim to fame. Author Jack London writes *The Call Of The Wild.* Buffalo Bill's Wild West Show plays in London.
1904, March 28			Future cowboy star, Charles Starrett aka The Durango Kid is born.
1904, Summer	Virgil and Allie Earp head for Goldfield, Nevada. It will be Virgil's last boom-town. Nellie Cashman opens a grocery supply house in Fairbanks, Alaska.		
1904, May 2			Crooner Bing Crosby is born.
1904, May 5			Playing for the Boston Pilgrims against the Philadelphia Athletics, "Cy" Young pitches the first perfect game in major league baseball.
1904, July 23			The ice crème cone is invented.
1904, September 1			Future movie cowboy, Johnny Mack Brown is born.
1904, Other Events			The New York City subway begins operations.
1905, February 15		Former New Mexico governor and Ben-Hur author Lew Wallace dies in Indiana.	

Date	Tombstone Events	Other Old West Events	Events Elsewhere
1905, May 16			Future actor Henry Fonda is born. He will later play Wyatt Earp in the 1946 movie, *My Darling Clementine*.
1905, October 19	Virgil Earp dies of pneumonia in Goldfield. Allie, as always, is at his side.		
1905, October 5			Future cowboy star Joel McCrea is born.
1905, December 24			Future industrialist Howard Hughes is born.
1905, Other events			Future B movie and television western star, Andy Devine is born. Future gambling Mecca, Las Vegas, NV is founded.
1906, January 5	Phin Clanton, brother to Ike Clanton and son of N.H. Clanton is killed near Globe, Arizona when his wagon team runs away with him. He is 61.		
1906, April 18	San Francisco experiences a major earthquake. Dr. George Goodfellow having an office and home in San Francisco loses everything.		
1906, April 29	George Parsons arrives in San Francisco with supplies to assist the homeless.		
1906, Other Events	Wyatt Earp meets typist John Flood who records his memoirs and makes an ill-fated attempt at Wyatt's biography. It is never published because the prose is so poor. Wyatt and Josie take up living in Los Angeles during the summer and in the desert town of Vidal during the winter. John Clum becomes the Postmaster for Fairbanks, Alaska. He will keep this position for three years.	With the success of 1903's "The Great Train Robbery", scores of western themed movies are produced.	Thomas Edison invents the "cameraphone", a device that synchronizes a phonograph and projector thereby adding sound to motion pictures.
1907, May 26			Future western star John Wayne is born .
1907, September 29			Future cowboy star Gene Autry is born.
1907, November 12	Earp patriarch Nicholas Porter dies in the old soldier's home in Sawtelle, CA.		

Date	Tombstone Events	Other Old West Events	Events Elsewhere
1907, Other Events			The Financial Panic of 1907 leads to the establishment of the Federal Reserve Act of 1913.
			The first Neiman-Marcus store opens in Texas.
1908, February 7			Future cowboy star Buster Crabbe is born.
1908, February 29		Wayne Brazel murders former New Mexico lawman, Pat Garrett near Las Cruces, NM.	
1908, March 22			Future author Louis L'Amour is born in North Dakota.
1908, May 20			Future actor James Stewart is born.
1908, November 6		Butch Cassidy and the Sundance Kid are killed in Bolivia.	
1908, Other Events			Henry Ford introduces his model T. It costs $850.
1909, February 17		Geronimo dies at 80 years old in Oklahoma.	
1909, March 24			Perhaps marking the start of a new breed of outlaw, Clyde Barrow of future Bonnie and Clyde fame, is born.
1909. April 1			A speed limit of seven miles per hour is imposed in Tucson, AZ.
1909, Other Events			3 million acres of western land are set aside for conservation purposes by President William Howard Taft.
			Railroad magnate E. H. Harriman dies at age 71.
			Artist Frederick Remington dies at 48. Although sometimes noted as being bigoted, Remington was one of the first members of the media to popularize and promote the Buffalo Soldiers.
			The Yuma Territorial Prison at Yuma, Arizona is closed.

Date	Tombstone Events	Other Old West Events	Events Elsewhere
1910, January 13			First public radio broadcast.
1910, April 20			Mark Twain dies at age 74.
1910, December 7	Dr. George Goodfellow dies from what was termed "multiple neuritis" although the real cause was never determined.		
1910, Other events	Tombstone businessmen John Dunbar and Richard Gird die. Gird purchased the original Tombstone mining claims from the Schieffelin Brothers.	Max Aronson, star of the first true western movie, *The Great Train Robbery* changes his name to Broncho Billy Anderson. He would go on to star in more than 370 movies.	The neon light is invented. Future "gun moll" Bonnie Parker is born.
1911, February 22		Outlaw Bill Miner and his gang rob a train near White Sulpher, Georgia. He is captured and returned to prison.	
1911, June 9		Prohibitionist Carrie Nation dies at age 64 in Kansas, nine years short of seeing her dream come true. National Prohibition will begin January 16, 1920.	
1911, Other Events			The first all-metal airplane is built.
1912, January 12		In a scene reminiscent of 25 years prior, a running gun battle in the streets of Phoenix ends in the capture of several outlaws. Fortunately, the city was made safe for the first annual Phoenix Auto Show that began three days later.	
1912, February 14	Arizona becomes the 48th state of the Union.		
1912, March 13		Ben Kilpatrick, the last active members of one of the last "old-west outlaw gangs", The Wild Bunch, tries to rob a train in Texas. He, and another gang member are killed in the attempt.	
1912, April 14			The Titanic sinks killing 1517 people.
1912, June 7 3:10AM	Former Cochise county Sheriff and superintendent of the Yuma Territorial Prison, Johnny Behan dies in Tucson, AZ. His occupation is listed as Commissary Manager.		
1912, June 19			American government establishes the 8 hour work day.
1912, August 23			Singer and dancer Gene Kelly is born.
1912, September	Belle Clum, John Clum's second wife, dies.		
1912, October 31			Future television and movie western star, Dale Evans is born.
1912, November 5			Future television and movie star, Roy Rogers is born.

Date	Tombstone Events	Other Old West Events	Events Elsewhere
1912, Other events	Attorney William Mclaury, brother to Frank and Tom McLaury, slain during the OK Corral gun battle dies. Atty McLaury had represented the Mclaury-Clantons against the Earps after the OK Corral incident.		Ragtime music spawns a dance craze characterized by names like the fox trot, camel walk, chicken scratch, and lame duck. This phenomenon will resurface 50 years later with the advent of rock-n-roll music. It will be characterized by names like the monkey, the mashed potato, the frug, and the swim.
			Zane Grey write *Riders Of The Purple Sage*.
1913, July 10			Temperatures reach an all-time high in California's Death Valley, a sizzling 134 degrees.
1913, November 2			Future actor Burt Lancaster is born. He will later portray Wyatt Earp in the 1957 movie, *Gunfight At The OK Corral*.
1913, Other Events	Former Tombstoner Buckskin Frank Leslie, last heard from as he headed to the Yukon gold fields in 1897 resurfaces working in a pool hall in San Francisco.		The then tallest building in the world at 60 stories, the F.W. Woolworth building, is completed. The five and dime giant pays for the building, $13.5 million, in cash.
			At the other end of the financial spectrum, Buffalo Bill's Wild West Show fails financially. Cody joins the Sell-Floto Circus and makes a movie starring himself and former Indian fighter General Nelson Miles.
1913, August 10			Future cowboy star Noah Beery Jr, is born.
1913, September 2		Outlaw Bill Miner dies while serving time in Milledgeville, GA prison. He is 67 years old.	
1913, Other events	Former Tombstone businessman and Tombstone's 2nd (appointed) mayor, William Harwood dies. Harwood's boarding house was opposite C.S. Fly's photo studio to form the alley where the O.K. Corral gunfight was actually fought. Doc Holliday was boarding at Harwood's at the time.		Future western movie star Alan Ladd is born.

Date	Tombstone Events	Other Old West Events	Events Elsewhere
1914, January 31	Lark Ferguson, better known as Pete Spence, alleged accomplice in the attempted assassination of Virgil Earp dies of pneumonia near Miami, Arizona. Total cost of the funeral is $72. He is 72 years old.		
1914, September 14			Television's "Lone Ranger", Clayton Moore is born.
1914, October	A 63 year old John Clum marries a 43 year old Florence Baker.		
1914, Other Events			Mack Sennett begins production of the first "full length" motion picture. Future actor of many westerns, Richard Widmark is born.
1915, Circa January		Former lawman Bill Tilghman forms the Eagle Film Company and begins shooting a western movie, *The Passing Of The Oklahoma Outlaws*.	
1915, February 12			Future patriarch of Bonanza's television ranch, The Ponderosa, Lorne Greene is born.
1915, February 15		Outlaw Frank James dies peacefully. He lived long enough to charge tourists 25 cents to take pebbles from brother Jesse's grave.	
1915, March 27		While directing his movie company's first western film, former lawman Bill Tilghman stops shooting to again strap on his .45's and join a posse after two bank robbers. He eventually caught one of the robbers, and then returned to his film.	
1915, May 7	Albert Bilicke, son of Tombstone businessman Gus Bilicke dies aboard the ill-fated "Lusitania".		
1915, September		Bill Tilghman shows his film, *The Passing Of The Oklahoma Outlaws*, at Tabor Palace in Denver.	
1915, Other Events	John Clum takes up date farming in southern California.		
1916, June 18			Future "Paladin" star, Richard Boone is born.
1916, October 12			Future cowboy star Glenn Ford is born.

Date	Tombstone Events	Other Old West Events	Events Elsewhere
1916, November 22			Author Jack London commits suicide. He is 40 years old.
1918, November 11			WW I ends.
1919, January 6			Former President, Rough Rider and lover of the cowboy culture, Teddy Roosevelt dies.
1916, February 21		The last member of the Younger Gang, Cole Younger dies at 72.	
1917, Other Events		Indian births exceed Indian deaths for the first time since before the Civil War.	
1919, May 26			Future actor Jay Silverheels, Tonto to Clayton Moore's *Lone Ranger*, is born.
1919, June 14			Future actor Gene Barry, TV's *Bat Masterson* is born, 2 years before the death of the real Bat Masterson.
1919, Other events	Charles Reppy, partners with John Clum and then full editor of the Tombstone Epitaph dies.		First municipal airport opens at Tucson, AZ.
			Future western character actor Slim Pickens is born.
			The name "Sunkist" is used for the first time for California grown fruit.
1920, January 16			The first day of Prohibition effectively kills what had been known for 50 years as the traditional saloon.
1920, February 18			Future western actor Jack Palance is born. He will be remembered for many movies and TV shows. But perhaps his most memorable will be "Curley" in the western comedy, *City Slickers* with comedian Billy Crystal.
1921, March 5			Future cowboy star Lash Larue is born.
1921, September 7			The first Miss America pageant is held.

Date	Tombstone Events	Other Old West Events	Events Elsewhere
1921, October 25		Former lawman turned New York sportswriter, Bat Masterson, dies at his desk at the Morning Telegraph. "The real story of the old west", Bat told young writer Stuart N. Lake, "can never be told unless Wyatt Earp will tell what he knows. And he isn't talking." Stuart N. Lake went on to publish "Wyatt Earp: Frontier Marshal in 1931, a pivotal point in the legend Wyatt Earp and the old-west has become.	
1921, Other Events		African-American cowboy and author Nat Love dies at 67 years old.	
1922, February 15	Former Cochise County Sheriff and noted cattle rancher, "Texas" John Slaughter dies in Douglas, Arizona. From the front porch of his beloved Arizona ranch, one can look straight into Mexico.		
1922, October 8			Future cowboy star Ben Johnson is born.
1922, Other events			The first commercially sponsored radio program is broadcast in New York on WEAF radio.
1923, February 13			Future aviator and first man to travel faster than the speed of sound, Chuck Yeager is born.
1923, March 2			The first issue of Time magazine appears.
1923, March 26			Future television lawman, James Arness aka Matt Dillon, is born. He will make "Gunsmoke" a household word.
1923, July 14			Future cowboy star Dale Robertson is born.
1923, September 10			Future cowboy star Rex Allen is born.
1923, Other events	Former Tombstone attorney Tom Fitch dies.		Jacob Schick patents the electric shaver.
			"The Covered Wagon" is one of the ten best films of the year and sets the stage for a genre of movie-making.
June 2, 1924		Native Americans gain US citizenship.	
1924, June 4			Future television and movie cowboy star, Dennis Weaver is born.

Date	Tombstone Events	Other Old West Events	Events Elsewhere
1924, June 20			Future war hero and movie star, Audie Murphey is born. He will portray former Tombstone mayor and San Carlos Indian Agent John Clum in the 1956 movie, "Walk The Proud Land".
1924, Other Events	"The Epitaph" newspaper surviving all others in the area becomes, again, "The Tombstone Epitaph". Wyatt Earp visits San Francisco. The Chronicle notes his arrival with the headline, "Terror Of Evildoers Is Here – Alive Because He Was Quick With A Trigger". *Info courtesy Casey Tefertiller – Wyatt Earp – The Life Behind The Legend*	At 71 years old, Bill Tilghman once again becomes a lawman at the request of Oklahoma Governor M. E. Trapp as the City Marshal for the city of Cromwell, OK. He begins by ridding the city of the criminal element, including a drug dealer. Tilghman was later killed when he confronted a drunken prohibition agent.	Mail now travels from New York to San Francisco via aircraft in under 28 hours.
1925, January 4	"Queen of the Camp" Nellie Cashman dies at 80 years old in Victoria, British Columbia.		
1925, January 9			Future actor and nemesis of Clint Eastwood's "Man With No Name", Lee Van Cleef is born in New Jersey.
1925, January 26			Actor Paul Newman born.
1925, April 19			Actor High O' Brian is born in Rochester, NY. He will later star in the television show, "The Life & Legend Of Wyatt Earp".
1925 November 28			The Grand Ole Opry has it's start as the WSM Barn Dance broadcast on Nashville radio station WSM. In 1927, the Saturday night show will change it's name to the Grand Ole Opry.
1925, December 6	Joe Bignon, showman, husband of "Big Minnie" Bignon, and former owner of the Bird Cage Theatre dies in Pearce, Arizona. His gravestone remains there today.		
1925 December 12			The nation's first motel, James Vail's Motel Inn with accommodations for 160 people opens in San Luis Obispo, CA.

Date	Tombstone Events	Other Old West Events	Events Elsewhere
1925, Other Events			Adolf Hitler publishes the first volume of "Mein Kampf".
			Electric coffee percolators are introduced.
1926, January 25	James Earp dies in Los Angeles and is buried in the Mt. View cemetery in San Bernardino.		
1926, March 16			Physics instructor Robert Goddard launches the first liquid fueled rocket marking the beginning of the space age.
1926, June 19		20,000 Indians converge on Little Big Horn in Montana to commemorate the battle that defeated General George Custer 50 years earlier.	
1926, November 3		Sharpshooter and performer, Annie Oakley dies at 66 years old. Her husband a business manager, Frank Butler, will die less than 3 weeks later.	
1926, Other Events	William B. Kelly assumes the editorship of The Epitaph. He realizes that the future of Tombstone is not in the flooded mines but in the climate and history of the town. After a visit with "Tombstone" author Walter Noble Burns, Kelly begins promoting Tombstone as a tourist attraction. Helldorado Days, still celebrated today, is Kelly's idea. Walter Noble Burns pens, *The Saga Of Billy The Kid*.		NBC, the National Broadcasting Company is established. The Army Air Corps is established.
1927, September 27			Philo Farnsworth transmits the image of a horizontal line across a room in his San Francisco laboratory and projects it on a screen marking the birth of television.
1927, September 30			Baseball great Babe Ruth hits his 60th home run of the season. The record will stand until another Yankee, Roger Maris, hits 61 in 1961.
1927, Other Events	The Tombstone Epitaph office moves from its original spot, across Fremont Street from the OK Corral, to its present location on Fifth Street occupying the former Ritchie's Dance Hall.		

104

Date	Tombstone Events	Other Old West Events	Events Elsewhere
1928, April 7			Future western star James Garner is born. He will later play Wyatt Earp in the 1967 film, *Hour Of The Gun*.
1928, September			Penicillin is discovered.
1928, July 30			The MGM lion roars for the first time.
1928, October 6			"The Jazz Singer" makes it's debut as the first film with spoken dialogue.
1928, November 18			Mickey Mouse first appears in the cartoon, "Steamboat Willie".
1928 Other events	Newton Jasper Earp dies and is buried in Sacramento, CA. "Helldorado", a book written by former Cochise County Under Sheriff, Billy Breakenridge is published. Breakenridge, once the subordinate to Cochise County Sheriff Johnny Behan slams the Earps.		First sound film, "The Lights Of New York" is released.
1929, January 13 Sunday, 8:05AM	Wyatt Earp dies in Los Angeles of prostate cancer. His last words were "Suppose…suppose…" Faithful to the end, his wife Josie is by his side. His death certificate lists his occupation as "Mining".		
1929, January 17			New York cartoonist Elzie Segar introduces Popeye, a spinach loving sailor.
1929, February 12		Actress and socialite Lilly Langtry dies in Monaco at 76 and is buried in her native Jersey Island in British Channel Islands.	
1929, June 17			Delta Air Service begins passenger flights between Dallas and Jackson, MS.
1929, June 27			Bell Labs in New York demonstrates an early color television set. The screen is the size of a postage stamp.
1929, October 24-27	The first "Helldorado Days" celebration is held in Tombstone celebrating the town's history and legend. Former Mayor John Clum attends and is horrified by the re-enactment of the famous OK Corral gunfight of 48 years ago calling the incident "repulsive and distressing".		

Date	Tombstone Events	Other Old West Events	Events Elsewhere
1929, October 29			The stock market crashes marking the beginning of The Great Depression, a financial and social malaise which will last until the start of World War II.
1929, December 13		Former cattle-baron Charles Goodnight dies at 93.	
1929, December 31			Beginning a tradition that will last for decades, Guy Lombardo and his Royal Canadians open at New York's Roosevelt Hotel. The radio broadcast is heard nationally.
1929, Other events		Actress Lillie Langtry dies.	The airship, "Graf Zeppelin" flies around the world in 20 days, 4 hours, 14 minutes. The movie version of *The Virginian* starring Gary Cooper is released.
1930, February 28		Former gambler and western luminary, "Poker Alice" Tubbs dies at 79 in Rapid City, South Dakota.	
1930, May 8	Walter & Edith Cole assume the Epitaph's assets. On the newspaper's mast-head they write, "The Spirit Of Tombstone Is To Never Say Die." The line is later embellished to say, "The Town Too Tough To Die".		
1930, May 31			Future western super-star Clint Eastwood is born in San Francisco.
1930, Other Events	Former Tombstoner Buckskin Frank Leslie moves to Seattle where he lives with his married daughter. He is 88 years old.		The average life expectancy is now 61 years.
1931, January 31	Behan confidant and later, the writer of a Tombstone expose' entitled "Helldorado" Billy Breckenridge dies in Tucson, AZ. He is 84.		
1931, February 8			50's teen idol and actor James Dean born.
1931, October	Stuart N. Lake's book, "Wyatt Earp Frontier Marshall" is released and is an instant hit starting the first of many "Earp-mania" waves.		Al Capone is jailed for tax evasion.
1931, Other Events			Gambling is legalized in Nevada.

Date	Tombstone Events	Other Old West Events	Events Elsewhere
1932, May 2 9:30AM	John Clum dies in Los Angeles of heart disease. He is 80 years, 8 months, and 1 day old.		
1932, Other Events	"Law & Order", the first movie version of the Tombstone saga stars Walter Huston as Frame Johnson, a Wyatt Earp rip-off, is released to theaters. Info courtesy Casey Tefertiller – Wyatt Earp – The Life Behind The Legend		The great Depression reaches it's lowest point. Wages are less than half of what they were in 1929 and 5000 banks have closed. Amid all the depression, Radio City Music hall opens in New York.
1933, January 5			Construction begins on the San Francisco Golden Gate Bridge.
1933, April 6		Elizabeth Bacon Custer, widow of the ill-fated George Armstrong Custer, dies in New York.	
1933, December 5			Prohibition ends.
1933, Other events	Tombstone diarist George W. Parsons dies. William Hunsaker, an attorney and friend of Wyatt's during his later years, dies. Hunsaker was one of the pall bearers for Wyatt.	The last Buffalo Bill dime novel appears marking the end of a six-decade phenomenon. The dime novel did more for the promotion of the old-west than any movie or book transcending the time from the start of the western frontier, through it's closing at the turn of the century to the beginning of the radio and movie western.	The first drive-in movie theater opens in NJ. Alcatraz becomes a federal prison.
1934, Other Events			Bank robber and murderer John Dillinger is shot to death by FBI agents. Outlaws Bonnie Parker and Clyde Barrow are shot to death by lawmen in Louisiana.
1935, July	Tombstone correspondent to the San Diego Union, Clara Spaulding Brown, dies in Los Angeles. She is 81 years old.		
1935, March 7		Former Denver socialite and wife of industrialist, Horace Tabor, "Baby Doe" Tabor is found frozen to death at the worthless Matchless Mine near Leadville, Colorado. Although the mine had been a windfall for Horace Tabor, it had not produced any silver to speak of in years. Despite this, Horace, on his death-bed, asked his wife never to sell the Matchless.	

Date	Tombstone Events	Other Old West Events	Events Elsewhere
1935, Other Events			Laura Ingalls Wilder writes, *Little House On The Prairie*.
1936, April 18		Singing cowboy, Gene Autry, records *Back In The Saddle Again*. It will become forever linked with him as his signature song.	
1937, July 5			Future cowboy star Robert Fuller is born.
1937	Former Tombstone attorney Allen English dies.		
1938, Other Events		Film-making comes to southeastern Arizona in a town called Gleeson, just a few miles from Tombstone. Paramount Pictures makes "The Mysterious Rider", a Zane Gray novel.	Orson Wells' "War Of The Worlds" is broadcast on radio. Many people panic thinking that earth is really being invaded by Martians.
1938, October 6	The Epitaph is purchased by Clayton Smith. Like his predecessor, John Clum, Smith tirelessly promotes the town and is in large part responsible for it's rebirth as a tourist attraction in the post war years.		
1938, December 16	Frederick James "Fred" Dodge, gambler and Wells Fargo undercover agent dies at Boerne, TX. He is 84 years old.		
1939, Other Events		Based on Stuart N. Lake's 1931 book, the movie "Frontier Marshall" is released starring Randolph Scott as Wyatt Earp.	Author Zane Grey dies at 69.
1940, Other events	Doc Holliday's paramour, Big Nose Kate, dies.		Matinee western star Tom Mix dies at 60 in a car accident near Florence, AZ.
1941-1945	Tombstone sees a brief resurgence with the increased military personnel at nearby Fort Huachuca.		
1941, February 16	Dr. Endicott Peabody, builder of Tombstone's St. Paul's church returns to Tombstone to preach in the same church he built. He is 84 years old.		
1941, Other events	Adelia Douglas Earp, sister to Wyatt, Virgil, and Morgan, dies and is buried in the Mt. View Cemetery in San Bernardino.		Japanese forces, plunging the US into WW II bomb Pearl Harbor.

Date	Tombstone Events	Other Old West Events	Events Elsewhere
1944, December 19 10:50AM	Josephine Sarah Marcus Earp, widow of Wyatt Earp dies in Los Angeles of heart disease. "Other conditions' listed on her death certificate indicate senility. Her "usual occupation" is listed as housewife. (A rather trite moniker for a legend.) Her body is taken to Westwood Memorial Park where it is cremated December 22.		
1944, Other events	Endicott Peabody, founder and builder of Tombstone's St. Paul's Church dies.		Howard Aiken, a mathematician invents the *Mark I*, an automatic calculator – the forerunner to the computer.
1945, January 26			Future film star Audie Murphey, then 20, who would become WW II's most decorated soldier distinguishes himself in action in France. He will later play the part of Tombstone Mayor John Clum in the1956 movie, *Walk The Proud Land*.
1945, February 23			Ira Hayes, an Arizona Indian helps raise the American flag on Iwo Jima in a triumphant moment for the American Indian.
1945, August 6			The "Enola Gay" drops the first atomic bomb on Hiroshima, Japan.
1945, Other events			The FCC sets aside 13 channels for commercial TV broadcasting.
1946, Other Events		"My Darling Clementine", a John Ford movie premiers with Henry Fonda starring as Wyatt Earp and Victor Mature as Doc Holliday. It is extremely inaccurate but successful at the box office.	Matinee western star, William S. Hart dies at 75 in Los Angeles.
1947, October 14			Chuck Yeager becomes the first person to break the sound barrier.
1947, November 17	Virgil's wife, Allie, dies. Her body is cremated and buried in a common grave with her sister-in-law, Adelia Earp at the Mountain View Cemetery in San Bernardino, CA. Her final resting place, only a few feet from brother-in-law, James Earp, is unmarked. She is the last surviving member of the immediate Earp family.		

Date	Tombstone Events	Other Old West Events	Events Elsewhere
1947, December 23			Bell Labs announces the invention of the transistor.
1948, March 19	Wyatt Earp would have been 100 years old on this date.		
1948, Other Events			Idlewild airport opens in New York. It is the world's largest (at that time). It will be renamed Kennedy airport in 1963.
1949, September 15			The *Lone Ranger* starring Clayton Moore in the lead role begins what would become a very successful run on television. The show is still seen today on cable networks.
1951, September 22		Jacob Horner, 96, the last surviving member of George Custer's ill-fated 7th Cavalry, dies. Had it not been for a shortage of horses, Horner would have accompanied Custer at the Little Big Horn 75 years earlier.	
1951, Other Events			Hopalong Cassidy and the Cisco Kid are popular television shows.
1952, Other Events			*High Noon*, starring Gary Cooper, one of the greatest western films of all time is released.
1953, Other Events		A remake of the 1932 movie "Law & Order" premiers starring future president Ronald Reagan as Wyatt Earp.	
1954, Other Events			Wild Bill Hickok starring Guy Madison is a popular TV show.
1955, September 6 Tuesday 8:30PM EST		"The Life & Legend of Wyatt Earp" with Hugh O' Brian in the lead role premiers on ABC television. The show's a hit lasting 6 years and starts another "Earp-mania" trend.	
1955, November		Iron Hail, the last surviving Indian of the Little Big Horn fight dies at the Pine Ridge reservation in South Dakota. He is 98.	
1956, Other Events	"Walk The Proud Land", a movie about John Clum during his years as an Indian Agent at San Carlos is debuted with war hero Audie Murphy playing the title role.		
1957, February 10			Laura Ingalls Wilder dies at age 90.

110

Date	Tombstone Events	Other Old West Events	Events Elsewhere
1957, October 16 8:30PM		Television series "Tombstone Territory" premiers starring Pat Conway as Sheriff Clay Hollister, Gil Rankin as Deputy Riggs, and Richard Eastham as Harris Claibourne. The series will last 2 seasons. Other TV westerns are popular during this period including *Have Gun Will Travel*, *Maverick*, *Tales Of Wells Fargo*, *Wagon Train*, and *Zorro*.	
1959, November 20	Virgil Edwin Earp, son of Newton Jasper Earp, famous for his appearance on the television quiz show, The $64,000 Question, dies at age 80. He claimed to have been born in Tombstone in 1879.		
1959, December 19		Walter Williams, 117 years old, and the last surviving veteran of the Civil War, dies.	
1959, Other Events		With television becoming more and more popular, and with the advent of color television, TV westerns are booming. *Bonanza*, *Bat Masterson*, and *Rawhide* debut. Despite doing many other types of movies, Rawhide will forever tag Clint Eastwood as a western hero.	
1960, Other Events		Riding on the wave of the popular TV westerns, the movie, *The Magnificent Seven* with an all-star cast is released. It will make stars of Yul Brenner, Robert Vaughn, James Coburn, Charles Bronson, Steve McQueen, and Eli Wallach.	
1961, September 6		"The Life & Legend of Wyatt Earp", a very successful television show with Hugh O' Brian in the lead role concludes its 6 year run culminating with the famous OK Corral shoot-out, a month short of the 80th anniversary of the original fight.	
1962, Other Events		Although the public's taste for the traditional western TV show is waning with the demise of shows like *The Life and Legend of Wyatt Earp*, *Bat Masterson*, and *Wanted Dead Or Alive*, future president Ronald Reagan begins a four-year stint as host of *Death Valley Days*.	
1964, Other Events		*Bonanza* becomes TV's top-rated show. For years to come, tourists will flock to the Lake Tahoe area to see where the series is filmed. In 2001, a "prequel" called *Ponderosa* will have a less then stellar success.	

Date	Tombstone Events	Other Old West Events	Events Elsewhere
1967, Other Events		*Hour Of The Gun* starring James Garner as Wyatt Earp premiers in theaters.	
1969, November 20		"Indian troubles" continue on the "western frontier" as Indians seize Alcatraz island to protest government policies.	
1969, Other Events			B western star Gabby Hayes dies.
1971, Other Events		The last surviving Indian to have fought in the Indian wars of the 1870's dies. He is 98 years old.	
1972, Other Events		Protesting treatment of Indians by the US government, a band of Indians marches on Washington D.C. and occupies the Bureau Of Indian Affairs.	William Boyd, TV's Hopalong Cassidy dies at age 77.
1973, January 16		Four-hundred million people all over the world watch the last original broadcast of *Bonanza* affirming that people still like westerns, and still have family values. The show is popular today on cable television, almost 30 years later.	
1973, February 27		Indian dissidents begin a 71 day occupation of the site of the 1890 massacre at Wounded Knee, South Dakota.	
1974, January 24		Shirley Plume become the first Native American to head the Bureau Of Indian Affairs.	
1984, September		*Little House On The Prairie* debuts on television, more than 10 years after the TV western was declared dead by TV execs.	
1975, September 1		The last episode of *Gunsmoke* airs on TV. It has run successfully for 20 years.	
1974, June	The Epitaph becomes a monthly publication devoted entirely to western history and is circulated nationally. It is also published in a local format with local and regional news.		
1975, February	Production of the local edition of The Epitaph is turned over to the Journalism Dept. of the University Of Arizona allowing the monthly edition more room to grow. The Epitaph is distributed to subscribers' worldwide.		
1978, Other Events		New legislation aimed at helping Native Americans is enacted by Congress.	
1979, June 11			Actor John Wayne dies of cancer.
1979, October	The 50th annual Helldorado Days celebration is held in Tombstone.		

112

Date	Tombstone Events	Other Old West Events	Events Elsewhere
1983, Other Events		The buffalo population in the US is estimated to be 50,000, up from the 1,000 or so estimated to have roamed the great plains only 80 years prior.	
1985, Other Events		Levi Straus becomes the world's foremost clothing manufacturer. Larry McMurty writes *Lonesome Dove*.	
1991, March 16	The Southern California Paraders Assoc. erects a gravestone to Morgan Earp in Colton's Hermosa cemetery. Originally interred at Colton's Mt. Slover cemetery, Morgan's body was exhumed and moved along with 11 others on November 27, 1892 when the railroad purchased the Mt. Slover cemetery land. Up to this point, Morgan's grave had not been marked.		
1991, Other Events		Actor Kevin Costner's *Dances With Wolves* wins and Academy Award for Best Picture.	
1993, December 25		The movie "Tombstone" starring Kurt Russell and Val Kilmer is released. It is an instant hit and will develop an almost cult following among Tombstone enthusiasts and re-enactors worldwide.	
1993, Other Events		Clint Eastwood's *Unforgiven* wins an Academy Award for Best Picture.	
1994, June		The movie "Wyatt Earp" is released with Kevin Costner in the lead role. The close timing of these two similar movies starts another tide of "Earp-mania" although Kurt Russell's Wyatt Earp and the movie *Tombstone* will be the decided favorite among old-west aficionados.	
1994, July 2		Hugh O' Brian reprises his role as Wyatt Earp in the made-for-TV western, Wyatt Earp: Return To Tombstone".	

113

Date	Tombstone Events	Other Old West Events	Events Elsewhere
1995, Other Events	Tombstone resident Jack Fiske writes and publishes a small pamphlet-sized book entitled *My Friend Doc Holliday by Wyatt Earp* as written by Jack Fiske in response to many of his Tombstone bookstore customers asking about a book of the same name as depicted in the movie *Tombstone*. In the movie Kurt Russell as Wyatt Earp gives the book to Val Kilmer as Doc Holliday as Holliday lays dying of tuberculosis. Historically, the event never happened. But Mr. Fiske's book adds even further to the mystique that is "Tombstone".		
1997, October 26	116 years after the OK Corral shootout and a month short of the 50th anniversary of her death, Allie's name, and birth and death dates are added to Adelia's gravestone thanks to the efforts of The Friends Of The Old West Social Club. The grave-site re-dedication is attended by almost 100 old west fans, including several Earp family members.		
1998, January 3		Television tries to bring westerns back to the small screen with the debut of *The Return Of The Magnificent Seven*. It stars veteran actors Ron Perlman, Eric Close, and Michael Biehn, best known in "old-west circles" as Johnny Ringo from the movie *Tombstone*. Original movie cast member, Robert Vaughn assumes the role of a Circuit Court Judge in the series' second episode. With westerns out of popular favor, *Magnificent Seven's* last episode is aired June 7, 2000.	
1999, August 15	Endicott Peabody, great grandson and namesake of the founder of Tombstone's St. Paul's Episcopal Church visits the church to attend services.		

114

Date	Tombstone Events	Other Old West Events	Events Elsewhere
2002, January 12	Virginia Ann Cooksey Earp, wife of Nicholas Earp and mother to James, Wyatt, Virgil, Morgan, and Warren Earp receives a gravestone at the Pioneer Cemetery in San Bernardino. The service is attended by about 250 people including many re-enactors along with relatives Don and Zack Earp.		
2002, October 20	Tombstone marks the end of its 73rd annual Helldorado Days celebration – another success – and another affirmation that the old west is still alive…	Calico Ghost Town in California, a former silver mining camp, prepares for their annual Halloween celebration.	A sniper with a high-powered rifle kills and injures innocent people in the Washington D.C area. (Also see 1881, December 28 11:30PM)

…AND THE LEGEND GOES ON….

115

The Perspective

Clips, Quips, And Musings On History

A Monument To Wyatt?: Consider that you can, today, visit the Washington Monument in Washington D.C. and climb it's many stairs to a breathtaking view at the top. It is interesting to note that construction of that building started the year Wyatt Earp was born, 1848.

Howdy Neighbor: Law-man, Billy Breakenridege b.1846, cow-boy, Frank McLaury b.1848, and newspaperman, John Clum b.1851 were practically neighbors at one time, all coming from New York.

19th - Century Crime Wave That Lasted For Years: A Wells Fargo Stage was robbed, on average, once every eight weeks for 48 years. And that was just the Wells Fargo line – not counting all the other stage lines operating between 1852 and 1900!

History Repeats Itself: In July 1863 the first military draft in the U.S. sparked riots in New York. About 100 years later, the Vietnam War, and the draft, would have a similar effect.

Dive-Dive!: For all those that thought submarine warfare was a convention of WW II, the February, 1864 sinking of a Federal ship in Charlestown Harbor by the submersible H.L. Hunley is a sobering thought.

Titanic Versus Sultana: Perhaps due to the emerging mass-media of its time, our fascination with a past that some people alive today can still remember, or knew people who could remember it, or perhaps because of a very popular movie, most people today are familiar with the sinking of the luxury liner, Titanic in April of 1912. A similar tragedy, only 47 years earlier almost to the day, and with similar loss of life (1700 souls) the sinking of the steamship Sultana carrying Union soldiers returning from prisoner of war camps, is largely forgotten.

And The Winner Goes To Boom-Boom: Today, we think of the Nobel Prize as something very distinguished and notable. People of great character and integrity win Nobel Prizes. It is interesting and perhaps ironic to note that in 1867, Alfred Nobel, the man who established the initial fund for the Nobel Prize, patented dynamite, an instrument capable of great destruction.

100 Years Of Rioting: A race-riot against Chinese erupted in San Francisco in July, 1869. The Chinese immigrants were willing to work hard for little money, only wanting to survive. Ninety-Eight years later, the Chinese population has been assimilated into the US culture and things are calm in the Chinese neighborhoods in America. However, in July, 1967, race-riots erupted in Detroit involving an African American culture that has existed in the US for over 200 years.

Milestones In Transportation: In the summer of 1869, the Central Pacific Railroad line and the Union Pacific met at Promontory Point, Utah to complete the first trans-continental rail line. The east and west coasts of the county were finally linked. It had taken 262 years to establish a foothold in the US (Jamestown, Virginia established summer 1607), find the west coast (Lewis and Clark expedition) and connect the two together via transportation. In the summer of 1969, only 100 years after east met west via rail, and only 9 years after the commitment to do so (President Kennedy's inaugural address of 1960) Neil Armstrong set foot on the moon connecting, via transportation media, two celestial bodies.

Past Meets Future: The real old west begins to mingle with the celluloid old west in 1870 when future actor and friend of Wyatt Earp, William S. Hart is born.

Whoa Nellie: At a time when most women were relegated to being housewives, schoolteachers or soiled doves, future Tombstone restaurateur and individualist, Nellie Cashman, together with her mother, opened a boarding house and restaurant in Nevada in 1872.

Play Ball: Today, we can enjoy the thrill and excitement of a big-league baseball game. In their own time, the Earps, Doc Holliday, and the entire cadre of Tombstone luminaries could have enjoyed much the same thing as National League Baseball was established in 1876. In those days the cry "Kill the Umpire" could have had dire consequences!

The Legend Begins: The legend that is "Tombstone" actually began in September 1877 when prospector Ed Schieffelin recorded his first mining claim in the Pima County courthouse. He called it "Tombstone"

The Harry Carey Connection: Future old-west actor Harry Carey was born in January, 1878, a year before the founding of Tombstone. Ironically, he appeared in a 1938 movie, *The Law West Of Tombstone*, portraying an era that existed at the time of his birth. More ironically, his son, Harry Carey Jr. played Marshal Fred White in the 1993 movie, *Tombstone*.

Headed For Destiny: In reviewing the Tombstone time-line, note that by 1878, the principal players in Tombstone's hey-day are starting to come together.

Walk Where They Fell: In the time-line, note the dates of the founding of many of Tombstone's points of interest; the OK Corral in 1879, the Oriental Saloon (now a clothing store) and Grand Hotel (now Big Nose Kates's), in 1880, and Schieffelin Hall and the Russ House in 1881. All of these places and more, including the world-famed Birdcage Theatre, can be visited in Tombstone today!

Irony of Ironies: On October 23, 1881, diarist George Parsons writes, "Rather monotonous. I hope this state of things won't continue long." Little does he realize at the time that he is three days away from Tombstone's destiny!

Wyatt Earp Stars As "Superman": Contrary to many popular western movies, the "good guy" and the "bad guy" rarely faced each other down in the "dusty street". The OK Corral incident on October 26, 1881 was one of the few exceptions, eight men facing each other out in the open. Ironically, Wyatt Earp was the only one that walked away without a scratch. In fact, despite his many brushes with danger, and living in a time where shooting were a common occurrence, Wyatt was never wounded!

The Un-Trial Of The Century: While many people would depict the legal proceedings following the OK Corral incident as a "trial", it was in fact only a hearing to determine if there was enough evidence to put the Earps and Holliday on trial for the murder of Billy Clanton and Frank and Tom McLaury.

Not A Minor Miner: In December, 1881, Tombstone mining entrepreneur Dick Gird sold his mining interests for two million dollars – two million dollars! That is over 1600 times the annual pay for the average miner. Some dug the holes, some made money.

Bullet-Proof Vests In Tombstone?: While performing an autopsy on cattle rustler Billy Grounds, in 1882, Tombstone's Dr. Goodfellow noted that some of the buckshot that had been fired into Ground's face had not penetrated a silk scarf worn around his neck. Later, in 1887 Goodfellow wrote a paper, "The Impenetrability Of Silk To Bullets" which was published in the Southern California Practitioner. Could this have been the foundation for bullet-proof vests?

Wyatt's Telephone Bill: Ordinarily, we think of receiving our monthly telephone bill as a "modern day" convention. Yet, considering that the Rocky Mountain Bell telephone Company was formed in 1883, consider that Wyatt Earp could have received a telephone bill 120 years ago! I wonder what a long distance call cost back then?

Bigger Is Not Necessarily Better: In 1884, the ten-story Home Life Insurance Building in Chicago becomes the world's first skyscraper utilizing the concept of hanging floors and walls on a steel-beam superstructure. This, theoretically, makes the height of skyscraper virtually limitless. This thinking would run virtually unabated until September 11, 2001 when terrorists slammed passenger jet-liners into two of the world's tallest buildings, the World Trade Center in New York.

The Same Ills: People of 100 years ago suffered many of the same social ills as we do today. A February 22, 1889 issue of a Topeka, Kansas newspaper reports that cigarettes are killing off "a good many promising boys", on July 4, 1888, Mattie Blaylock, Wyatt's second wife was found dead of a drug overdose, and Rodney O' Hara becomes a victim of police violence at the hands of then-lawman Pete Spence on August 6, 1886.

More Extension Cord Please: In 1892, the first electric automobile was seen in America. In 2002, 110 years later, manufacturers are still trying to perfect it!

Just Say No To Metrics: In 1893, attempts to have the US change over to the metric systems fails. A similar attempt 70 years later will end the same way.

The Book Or The Movie?: In 1895, H.G. Wells published one of his best works, "The Time Machine" which could have been read by Wyatt Earp in his lifetime. I waited for the movie 65 years later.

A Strange Connection: Q. What do former New Mexico governor Lew Wallace, outlaw Billy The Kid, and NRA president Charlton Heston have in common? A. Billy The Kid, while incarcerated for crimes during the Lincoln County War was seeking clemency from then-New Mexico governor Lew Wallace, who was also the author of Ben-Hur, later made into a movie made famous by Charlton Heston.

1903 to 1993: "The Great Train Robbery", one of the first westerns was produced in 1903. Ninety years later, the movies "Wyatt Earp" and "Tombstone" are equally successful continuing to validate the premise that Americans love the "Old-West" genre.

Wyatt Earp Meets Captain Kirk: Wyatt Earp probably wasn't present when, on March 16, 1926, physics instructor Robert Goddard launched the first successful liquid fueled rocket marking the beginning of the space age. But consider that the same man who was present at the most famous shoot-out in the old west, was alive at the time of the first rocket launch!

Time Travel

May 1804: Explorers Lewis and Clark leave St Louis for the west coast. The entire trip will take over 2 years, or, on average, a year to travel "cross-country" one-way. Put another way, Lewis and Clark traveled at an average of a little less than one mile per hour.

June 1848: It now takes about 3 months to go from New York to San Francisco via ship to Panama, across the isthmus, then via ship to San Francisco. This equates to about 3 to 5 miles per hour.

October 1858: The first Overland Mail stage arrives in St Louis from San Francisco making the trip in 23 days, 4 hours. Another stage running in exactly the opposite direct made the trip in 24 days, 20 hours. This equates to about 6 miles per hour.

Summer 1865: In the summer of 1865, a 17 year old Wyatt Earp (some sources say this was actually Virgil) gets a job driving stage between San Bernardino and Los Angeles – it is a 6 hour trip each way and Wyatt makes one round trip each day. This equates to about 12 – 13 miles per hour. Today (2002) depending on the time of day, the time to make that same trip has only been cut by half, three hours out, and three hours back.

1869: By 1869, one could travel from New York to San Francisco via rail in about eight days. Allowing for stops for passengers, freight, and fuel, this equates to about 26 miles per hour.

1893: In 1893, people traveled to the 1893 World's Columbian Exposition in Pullman cars (railroad) traveling at 80 miles per hour. Going from San Francisco to Chicago now took a little over 3 days. A trip from New York to Chicago took a mere 26 hours.

October 14, 1947: Chuck Yeager is the first man to break the sound barrier. Flying over California he records a top speed of Mach 1.07 or 650 miles per hour. At that rate, theoretically, one can fly from St Louis to San Francisco in a little over 2 hours!

Today: Today, a trip from one coast to the other can be made in about 4 ½ to 5 hours, in the luxury and comfort of a modern jet-liner, traveling at almost 500 miles per hour.

Boom-Town "Baby-Boomers"

Living in America, and being exposed to so much advertising, we are constantly reminded of such demographic divisions as the Baby-Boomers (those born between about 1947 and 1961), Generation X, Generation Y, and so forth. As I started to record the birth dates for many of those people related to Tombstone I started to realize that these were the Baby-Boomers of the 19th century. Consider the following;

Name	Birth Year	Approximate Age At Time Of OK Corral Gunfight
James Earp	1841	40
Virgil Earp	1843	38
Nellie Cashman	1844	37
Johnny Behan	1845	36
Billy Breakenridge	1846	35
Frank McLaury	1848	33
Wyatt Earp	1848	33
C.S. Fly	1849	32
Alvira Earp (Virgil's wife)	1849	32
Johnny Ringo	1850	31
George W. Parsons	1850	31
Nellie Cashman	1850	31
Morgan Earp	1850	31
Doc Holliday	1851	30
Mayor John P. Clum	1851	30
Tom McLaury	1853	28
Fred Dodge	1854	27
Warren Earp	1855	26
Dr. George Goodfellow	1855	26
Milt Joyce (owner Oriental saloon)	1857	24
Billy Claibourne	1860	21
Josephine Marcus Earp	1861	20

Although sometimes portrayed by older actors in movies and television shows, most residents of Tombstone were rather young in 1881. Here is a brief look at some of the actors that have portrayed Tombstone citizens of 1881, and their ages at the time the movie or TV show was made.

	Actor's Birth Year	Year Movie Or TV Show Premiered	Age Of Actor At Time Of Movie Or TV Premiere	Age Of Actual Person At Time Portrayed (circa 1881)
Kevin Costner as Wyatt Earp	1955	1994 (Wyatt Earp)	39	33
Dennis Quaid as Doc Holliday	1954	1994 (Wyatt Earp)	40	30
Kurt Russell as Wyatt Earp	1951	1993 (Tombstone)	42	33
Val Kilmer as Doc Holliday	1959	1993 (Tombstone)	34	30
Bill Paxton as Morgan Earp	1955	1993 (Tombstone)	38	31
Sam Elliot as Virgil Earp	1944	1993 (Tombstone)	49	38
Michael Biehn as Johnny Ringo	1956	1993 (Tombstone)	37	31
Powers Booth as Curley Bill	1949	1993 (Tombstone)	44	30 approx.
Jason Priestly as Billy Breakenridge	1969	1993 (Tombstone)	24	34
Harry Carey Jr as Fred White*	1921	1993 (Tombstone)	72	30 approx.
Terry O'Quinn as Mayor Clum	1952	1993 (Tombstone)	41	30
Dana Delany as Josephine Marcus Earp	1956	1993 (Tombstone)	37	21
Jason Robards as Doc Holliday	1922	1967 (Hour Of The Gun)	45	30
James Garner as Wyatt Earp	1928	1967 (Hour Of The Gun)	39	33
Kirk Douglas as Doc Holliday	1918	1957 (Gunfight At The OK Corral)	39	30
Burt Lancaster as Wyatt Earp	1913	1957 (Gunfight At The OK Corral)	44	33

	Actor's Birth Year	Year Movie Or TV Show Premiered	Age Of Actor At Time Of Movie Or TV Premiere	Age Of Actual Person At Time Portrayed (circa 1881)
Hugh O'Brian as Wyatt Earp	1925	1955 (*The Life & Legend of Wyatt Earp*)	30	33
Victor Mature as Doc Holliday	1916	1946 (*My Darling Clementine*)	30	30
Henry Fonda as Wyatt Earp	1905	1946 (*My Darling Clementine*)	41	33
Randolph Scott as Wyatt Earp-type character	1898	1939 (*Frontier Marshal)*	41	33

When Did The "Old West" End?

At what point did the "old-west" cease to exist?

Many historians, and most old west re-enactors agree that the "old-west" period lasted from 1865 to 1900, a scant 35 years. For some this may be true. But for others, time, and the old west, are relative concepts.

In 1881, young visionary and artist Frederick Remington realized that the west, as he then knew it, would soon change and change forever. At 19, he began capturing on canvas and in sculpture a time that that was moving rapidly.

Wyatt Earp may have had a few more scrapes after leaving Tombstone, but for him, the end of his "vendetta ride" on April 8, 1882 when he and his posse arrived in Silver Spring, Colorado may have marked the end of his "old-west" days. Or did his "old west" day follow him to Dodge City in 1883?

John Clum lived through Tombstone's most turbulent times as its Mayor and premier newspaperman. Amid all the violence of that time, Clum always remained the optimist – always thought that Tombstone would be the hub of commerce and activity in Arizona. Because of his affiliation with the Earps and Holliday, who lost popular favor after the OK Corral incident, Clum lost his political clout. He sold his newspaper in May, 1882 and left Tombstone in June. He returned in 1885 for a brief period as a Postmaster but by his own admission, the "old Tombstone" didn't exist anymore. So for Clum, perhaps his "old west" days ended in June of 1882.

Yet another visionary and showman, William F. Cody staged his first "Wild West Show" on May 1, 1883 wanting to capture his visualization of the west that he had known, and knew was changing. Perhaps for Buffalo Bill, the real old west ended that day, and the "show version" began.

The 1890 US Census noted over 11,000,000 living west of the Mississippi River, 50,000 in Los Angeles and over 100,000 in Denver. By the US Census definition, 2 persons per square mile, the western frontier, that is, the "old west" no longer exists. But that was a scholarly and statistical definition. Cowboys and outlaws and romanticists didn't care much for statistics.

In 1893, Frederick Jackson Turner read his paper, "The Significance of the American Frontier in American History" at the World's Columbian Exposition in Chicago. In it, he announces that the "frontier is gone", echoing the word of the US Census Bureau in 1890. There were those who didn't believe him and made the "old west" last a little longer.

The people of Cheyenne, Wyoming marked the end of the "old-west" era in August of 1897 when, recognizing a mark in the annals of time, they put on the first "Frontier Days" celebration, remembering days gone by.

As early as 1898, before the days of Hollywood, movies depicting the "old-west" were being cranked out on the east coast for audiences hungry for adventure. While most were recognizing the end of the "old west" as it was known, the "old-west" era was just beginning for the moving picture industry with early stars like Tom Mix and William S. Hart.

In April, 1902, the first moving picture theater opened in Los Angeles and western movies are popular. Ironically, "western's" were being produced in movie studios on the east coast for consumption on the west coast.

But nobody told outlaw Bill Miner that the old west was closed! Recently released after serving 20 years in San Quentin prison for robbery, in September, 1903, Bill pulled another train robbery in Portland, Oregon. The old west lasted a little longer for Bill but his days were numbered.

In November, 1908, Butch Cassidy and the Sundance Kid were killed in Bolivia by Federales after supposedly pulling off several robberies. The "old west" lasted a little longer in underdeveloped countries… or… did it necessarily need to be an underdeveloped country to continue train robbing?

In March, 1912, Ben Kilpatrick, the last active members of one of the last "old-west outlaw gangs", The Wild Bunch, tried to rob a train in Texas. He, and another gang member were killed in the attempt marking the end of their "old west" days.

Three years later, while directing his movie company's first western film, former "old west" lawman Bill Tilghman stopped shooting to again strap on his .45's and join a posse after two very-real bank robbers. He eventually caught up with one of the robbers. But during the resumption of filming, spectators weren't sure if the movie action being filmed was "real", or movie acting. The end of the old west was truly blurred for Bill Tilghman.

It was about this time that moving pictures were coming into-their-own and westerns were popular sparking the careers of many early movie stars. Even Wyatt Earp served as a consultant for many movies and became fast-friends with movie-star William S. Hart. The movies of those days, as western-themed movies today, keep the old west alive for many.

As I complete this portion of the book, it is late August, 2002, and we are looking forward to visiting Tombstone in October for the 73rd annual Helldorado Days celebration. For some of us, the "old west" is not a geographic place on a map or a section of time marked by a calendar. For some of us, the "old west" is a place in the heart, a state-of-mind. It is a knowledge of people and events that marked a glorious and romantic period   It is a genre that is truly American yet, is recognized by people all over the world. The "old west" has no end… and no beginning… it just is.

Happy Trails…..

Photo Gallery

From a postcard circa late 1930's. Note the date on the sign, September 26, 1881, quite an error on a sign right outside of Tombstone. The correct date, of course, is October 26, 1881.

INTERIOR OF HISTORIC BIRD CAGE THEATRE

Although smaller than one might expect, the Bird Cage provided Tombstone citizens with laughter and entertainment for many years.

Card games were conducted in the lower, or basement floor of the Bird Cage and would go on seemingly indefinitely.

The world-famous Crystal Palace Saloon, seen here circa 1949-1950 was a favorite "watering hole" for many of Tombstone's luminaries. You can still step up to the bar and order a cold one, just as they did in 1881.

The Cochise County Courthouse, seen in this circa early 1930's photograph, still stands and is now a fascinating museum operated by the US Park Service.

Once a roaring show-place that ran 24 hours a day, this circa late 1920's photo makes it seem like the famous Bird Cage has hit the end of the trail. However, it has found new life as a museum which you can visit today.

Just imagine Curley Bill and Johnny Ringo watching a show, and firing their pistols into the ceiling as a sign of appreciation! They may have shown their dissatisfaction with a performer by firing in his/her direction! The ceiling and stage-front are both riddled with bullet holes, still visible today!

The lobby of the Bird Cage served as a coffee shop, circa early 1930's.

Ironically, this 1930's era postcard says Main Street when this is really Allen Street in Tombstone, looking east from 5th to 4th Street. On the right side of the street right about where the two telephone poles stand is what was the Grand Hotel and is now the site of Big Nose Kate's Saloon.

Here is another view of Tombstone's famed Allen Street looking west from 6th Street, or what used to be the "red light" district.

John Phillip Clum, Tombstone's most famous mayor and newspaper editor, seen here in a scan from an original C.S. Fly photograph taken about 1881.

His newspaper, The Tombstone Epitaph, founded May 1, 1880, is still published today.

If you find yourself in Tombstone, stop by the office on Fifth Street, and pick up a copy.

Here, from a postcard photo is the famed Tombstone Epitaph office located on Tombstone's Fifth Street between Allen and Fremont Streets, circa late 1920's, about the time that the Epitaph moved into this location. This was formerly Ritchie's Dance Hall.

M. E. Fly, Souvenir, Tombstone, Ariz.

Ed Schiefflin's Monument, Tombstone, Arizona

Molly Fly, wife of Tombstone photographer, C.S. Fly, was an accomplished photographer in her own right. Here is an early postcard with photos from Molly showing Tombstone's founder, Ed Schieffelin, and the monument erected to him, located just west of Tombstone city limits.

Virgil Earp's former residence at 528 H Street in Colton still stands today.

The community of Colton is still very much aware of how the Earps are interwoven into their town's history. Virgil served as the town's first law-man and patriarch Nicholas Porter Earp was the Justice of the Peace.

Grave site of John P. Clum located in the Resthaven area, Block 321, Interment Space 5 of the Forest Lawn Memorial Park in Glendale, California.

Grave site of Morgan Earp at the Hermosa Cemetery in Colton, only a few blocks away from Virgil's former home.

Appendix

Have Bar Will Travel

It's back stands over nine feet tall, typical of many of it's type in it's time. It is over twenty feet long, plenty long enough to accommodate many a thirsty patron. And it has traveled thousands of miles, an unlikely feat for something so huge! But not improbable when you consider that Wyatt Earp himself likely dispensed beer, wine, and other spirits from behind it's mahogany facade: the bar from Wyatt Earp's Tonopah, Nevada, Northern Saloon.

Originally built in 1894, the bar spent its first years in Virginia City, Nevada during that city's silver revival period.

In 1901, Al Martin purchased the bar for a new saloon and gambling hall in the mining district of Tonapah, Nevada. Fresh from his adventures in Alaska, and flush with money looking for another investment, Wyatt Earp backed Martin in the Northern Saloon. While Martin managed the saloon, Wyatt and wife Josie would take many prospecting excursions in the surrounding mountains. But, no doubt, there were times when Wyatt threw a beer or two over the bar.

In 1903, partners Martin and Earp relocated the Northern Saloon to nearby Goldfield, Nevada taking the bar with them.

In 1905, possibly after the death in October of Wyatt's brother Virgil, who served as a lawman in Goldfield, the Martin/Earp partnership ended and the contents of the Northern, including the bar, were sold.

The bar's history is somewhat hazy at this point. There is some indication that it next saw service at the Mayflower Saloon in Beatty, Nevada and other information placing it at the Monaco Saloon in nearby Rhyolite. One source notes that in 1910, the bar was moved from a failing Rhyolite to Las Vegas and the Arizona Club where it remained until the late 20's to early 30's when it was returned to Rhyolite. However, an inscription on the back of the bar's back section states:

```
Death Valley Curley
Box 126  Beatty N.V.

Mooved this bar from the old Mayflower club
In Beatty, To: Ryolite Nev.  Sept. 16, 1937 For
Mr. Wess Moreland and in stalled it in
The old depot at Ryolite Nev.

Virgil Colvin          helped
Frank Kennedy
```

The inscription above, written as it appears on the bar indicates that a Wess Moreland now owned the bar. To be precise, the new owner was a Norman Westmoreland who operated a "road house" at the former Ryolite railroad depot from 1937 until his death in 1948.

Upon the death of Westmoreland, the property, along with the bar passed to his sister, a Frederica Heisler. Married to a minister, and being a very religious person Mrs. Heisler was appalled to discover she had inherited a "bawdy house" which she immediately closed. Realizing however, the historical significance of the place, she reopened the building as a museum. Over time, needing additional living funds at various times, she began to sell off pieces of the estate.

Mrs Heisler died in 1983 and the estate sold. The fate of the bar from 1983 to 1991 is presently unknown. But in 1991, the bar was moved to the Bella Union in Tombstone where it remained until it was removed to Rancho Mirage, California in the fall of 1998.

Despite it's long history, the bar is in remarkably good shape. One of the two nearly 10 foot long back mirrors is still original, the other being damaged sometime during the 30's. Unlike most bars of this era that have been painted over, this bar has seen only a few coats of varnish, the decals showing that the bar was union-made are still intact as is the patent number plate. As if in defiance of it's age, or to proudly show it's heritage, the manufacturer's name; Brunswick, Balke and Collander Company is still clearly visible on the bar's face.

The upper left column on the bar-back shows evidence of a burn, likely inflicted by an oil lamp hung too close to the column. Along the top of the bar-back are a series of small holes inflicted by tacks used to hang coyote tails, the hunting trophies of Norman Westmoreland and friends.

On Thanksgiving weekend in 1905, a lover's triangle erupted in a gunfight between the Monaco Saloon's bartender and his lover's husband. The husband burst into the Rhyolite's Monaco Saloon, six-shooter drawn and began firing at the bartender. The first shot from the husband went low and glanced off the bar front's mahogany face; about elbow high. The bar still retains the scar left by the .44 slug.

The bartender, ducking behind the bar returned fire from a crouched position not even knowing if he was firing upon patron or perpetrator. Unable to see the bartender, but figuring where he was from the position of his pistol-firing hand, the husband shot straight into the bar's lower face, killing the bartender. The hole made by the fatal bullet has since been repaired, but like an old wound, it's scar is still evident.

As was last known, the bar is the pride of Jeff and Cindy Moroni, and the center-piece of their antique store, the Antique Outpost in Rancho Mirage, California, located on Route 111 just east of Palm Springs.

John P. Clum – A Life

Ordinarily, when most people think of the old west and the people and that populated it, they think of people like Wyatt Earp, immortalized by a 30-second street brawl in Tombstone. They think about William F. (Buffalo Bill) Cody – master showman, true pioneer and, if not for whom, the old-west might have died with the turn of the twentieth century. They think of Butch Cassidy and the Sundance Kid, commemorated by Paul Newman and Robert Redford in their famous 1969 movie of the same name. They think of Billy The Kid, again, the subject of so many Hollywood movies.

The west wasn't all men. The average person might remember Martha Jane Canary aka Calamity Jane, Belle Starr, or Lilly Langtry although they may not remember why these women were noted. Those of the baby-boomer generation might also mention Annie Oakley, although they are not sure if she was a real person or the fruit of some television writer, portrayed by actress Gail Davis.

But there were many more people that populated the west – the countless cowboys, miners, business people, shop-keepers, entrepreneurs, soiled doves and many others who were part of a time and place in history, and whose accomplishments have been long forgotten.

Somewhere between celebrities like the Wyatt Earps and Calamity Jane's of the world, and the ubiquitous yet forgotten shopkeepers and dance hall girls whose stories will never be told, there lie those whose lives that are remembered by a precious few.

It is therefore incumbent upon those who still remember to keep those names and those stories alive. Here, told in the first-person, is the story of one of those little-known, unsung, yet infinitely important people from the old west – John P. Clum.

Clum is best known for two things. First, as the first elected mayor of Tombstone serving during 1881, the height of Tombstone's hey-day. And second, he is known as the founding editor of the Tombstone Epitaph newspaper, an enterprise that his detractors thought would not last six months but is still enjoyed today be readers all over the world.

Here then, told in the first person, is a brief story of Clum's life.

November 15, 1929

A Reflection

Even at my present age of 78, I am not given to bouts of
melancholy as several of my contemporaries are bound to do. Nor
do I often have thoughts of the past and wish for other times as
I pride myself on being a forward thinker. However, recent
events have caused me to take a look around myself, and take a
look back at where I have been.

This does not indicate a sadness or longing, but rather an
assessment of a life long-lived when so many of my friends and
colleagues have passed on. Reppy, my former business partner
passed on back in '19. My dear sister Jane crossed over in '22.
Another dear friend and former Tombstoner, Nellie Cashman barely
lived to see the start of 1925. And, perhaps the greatest
Tombstoner of them all, Wyatt Earp, passed on earlier this year.

Tombstone – perhaps that is the cause of my wandering thoughts at
this late hour of the day in the late hour of life. I have just
recently returned from that old mining camp where they celebrated
what was called the first "Helldorado Days", a commemoration of
Tombstone's first 50 years. It was good to see so many old
faces, even faces of my former adversaries including Billy
Breakenridge. But most of them are gone now – all gone.

But other events, current events, remind me that my time on earth
is getting short. The stock market crash of a few weeks ago is
sending a panic across the country, not unlike the events of
1893. But this time, it seems different, more widespread, more
invasive to the lives of everyone and it worries me so.

Perhaps now is a good time, before all memories fade away, to
make some notes on my life.

John Phillip Clum - A Life

I was born September 1, 1851 near Claverack, New York in the Hudson River Valley. Being the baby of the family was not always easy. My older brother George and sisters Cornelia and Jane were, at the time, a source of constant teasing. These days, I take solace in the knowledge that Cornelia and George are still around, Jane having passed on back in '22.

I had, by most accounts, a normal boyhood and did relatively well in school. Mother and father thought I should further my education and I became a student at Rutgers University in New Jersey in 1869. The school was operated by the Dutch Reformed Church, to which I paid little attention. That is, until several years after I left the school.

Looking for excitement beyond the normal collegiate studies, I engaged in school athletics, playing what was then new game called football. Being that it was in its infancy, the game had quite a crudeness to it. We would run about the field for an hour, making goals as we could. And at the end of it all, we weren't sure who the winner was.

At the conclusion of my freshman year, I knew I wanted more adventure than Rutgers could provide and so I left. I next found myself with the Army Signal Corp in Santa Fe, New Mexico watching the weather and reporting back to Washington via daily telegraph. That was September 1871; a refreshing departure from east-coast culture. But I was always in fear of Indian attacks.

It was about this time that President Ulysses S. Grant introduced a peace policy toward the Indians. Rather than try to eradicate the landscape of the savages in favor of manifest destiny, Grant thought it better to control them by placing them on reservations. He also thought it best to have the reservations overseen by members of religious groups, being that the US Army had forever made mortal enemies of the Indians in their efforts to exterminate them. It was on that premise that the Office of Indian Affairs went to Rutgers, looking for new Indian Agents. I, of course, was not there. But my friends remembered my adventurous spirit, and love of a challenge, and placed my name in the hat so to speak. And besides, I was already in "the west".

In August, 1874, I arrived at the San Carlos Indian Reservation as the new Indian Agent. Never had I faced a more daunting, yet fascinating challenge. The former Indian Agent, and an Army Lieutenant had been killed in an uprising by the Apaches some time prior.

Gross mistreatment at the hands of the US Army had taken their toll and the feeling by Indians, military personnel and reservation civilians was tense to be sure. To try to defuse the issue, I knew I had to eliminate, or at least reduce, the military presence. To that end I introduced the concept of Indian self-rule and formed the Indian Police and Indian Tribunal. The Tribunal would define laws and mete-out punishment and the Indian Police would enforce the law.

The Apaches embraced the concept and came to call me Nantan-Betunnykahyeh, or, Boss With The High Forehead. Although only 22 years of age at the time, my hairline had begun receding very early and I already was worthy of such a sobriquet.

My plan worked so well that by October, 1875, I was able to force the Army off the reservation and I lived on the reservation with the Apaches and a few other civilians.

In the summer of 1876 I wanted to take a trip east to see friends and family and thought it would be a good idea to bring a few Apaches to put on a "Wild West" show, giving the easterners a taste of Arizona Territory. By today's standards, you might say I was a man ahead of time (except for Col. Cody) putting on re-enactments for the easterners. But the idea went over badly being that Lt. Col. George Custer and his entire military force was wiped out at the Little Big Horn only weeks before. The sentiment, especially in Washington, was very anti-Indian and nobody wanted to see them, civilized or not.

But the trip east was by no means a total failure. After visiting the Centennial Exposition in Philadelphia, I returned with my Apache charges as far west as Colorado where a pre-arranged group of teamsters would see that they found their way back to San Carlos. I turned around and headed east again to Ohio where, on November 8, 1876, I married Mary Dennison Ware.

But my Apaches would soon find another way to distinguish themselves. Geronimo, the renegade had again run off the San Carlos reservation. Reports reached us at San Carlos that he and small band were looting and plundering ranchers in a far-reaching area. It became my responsibility to capture and return him to the reservation. Who better to capture an Apache, than other Apaches. We tracked him all the way to New Mexico where we were able to capture him at gunpoint. I suppose he did not want to start a gun-battle with his own people. It was the only time he was ever captured at gunpoint. He escaped to cause depredations on several other occasions but was always thereafter captured by negotiation.

When I first started at San Carlos I was in charge of about 400 Apaches. As the Army became more adept at capturing them, and word of my success became spread, more and more Apaches joined the reservation until, by the summer of 1877, I was now in charge of 5,000 Apaches with no raise in pay and little support from the government. Continued letters to the Office of Indian Affairs for more money for myself and more supplies for my charges went unheeded and I suppose, un-read. I decided then that it was time to move on.

I then moved on to what was then the booming city of Tucson where I went into the legal profession and newspaper publishing business with the "Arizona Citizen" newspaper. The work was steady, albeit, no more profitable than being an Indian Agent. And although I no longer was required to endure the indignities of low pay and the monumental work at San Carlos, after being in charge of 5,000 Indians, and capturing Geronimo at gunpoint, the prospect of earning my living behind a desk seemed overly tame and distasteful to me. I needed more excitement.

Mary presented me with a little excitement; a baby boy, Henry Woodworth Clum! Our first child died in infancy so we were naturally overjoyed with Woodworth!

Then, reports began to come in about a new mining camp about 50 miles south and east of Tucson in what was then called the Tombstone mining district. A man named Ed Schieffelin, a civilian working out of nearby Camp Huachuca had found a silver vein there back in '78. Together with his brother, Ed, and with the help on financier, Richard Gird, they were pulling ton after ton of rich ore from the ground.

In December of '79, I rode down there to see what all the excitement was about. The town, if you could call it that, was still a collection of tents, hastily built wooden houses and shanties. But it also had the Alhambra Saloon, Cosmopolitan Hotel, Brown's Hotel, and a host of mercantile stores, miner's supply houses, boarding houses, and, of course, several drinking establishments. The town was growing every day and the silver ore coming from the ground around it looked like it was rich and plentiful. It had all the makings of a boomtown, a place where a man could not only prosper, but also find excitement and opportunity that only a boomtown can provide.

As I rode back to Tucson, my mind was already made up! In February, 1880, I sold my interest in the "Citizen" and headed to Tombstone!

Upon my arrival in Tombstone, I had to find a way to make a living. Already, several lawyers had "hung out a shingle". In a place where so much money changes hands, there is a need for lawyers. But I could not envision myself as a frontier orator. I wanted something more - a chance to steer the destiny of a new city and have far-reaching influence. Another newspaper held the answer I then thought!

But a newspaper, the "Nugget" already existed having been established in October of '79. Of course, in politics, and Tombstone was a very political city then as it is now, a differing view is always needed. And so, I decided to start another newspaper and sent for a printing press and other supplies.

But what to call a newspaper in a city named Tombstone? It became a macabre dilemma. In talking with other prominent business people, somebody quipped, "every tombstone needs an epitaph" - Tombstone Epitaph. I liked it! It was a name both witty and fitting - as long as one had a sense of humor. My detractors called the name silly to disgusting. They claimed that such a morbid name would force the paper into oblivion within months. I am happy to report that although not in its original home (as that building has all but fallen down) the Tombstone Epitaph is still alive and well, 49 years later!

From that point, things began to look up. By July, the Epitaph that had started as a weekly had become a daily newspaper with so much now happening in town. The town also began to splinter into two factions; those that supported the cow-boys (there were so many of them and they were good business being able to consume severe quantities of liquor and food) and those that supported the Earp brothers and the business owners in town. The Nugget chose to support the cow-boys while my Epitaph supported the Earp point of view. It was also about this time that I took on the task of Postmaster for the newly established post office at Tombstone. Little did I know at that time that it would lead to a career that would support me for many years.

People of all ranks continued to pour into Tombstone. By the end of 1880 it was apparent that Tombstone had outlived its station as a village and a city charter was enacted.

On January 4, 1881 the first elections were held under the city charter. I had no intention of running for anything in that first election, let alone mayor. But the Republican candidate pulled out at the last minute. Wanting a candidate to oppose an unpopular Democrat, my friends, including one of my biggest supporters, George W. Parsons, made me a candidate for the office of Mayor.

Perhaps Parsons threw my name in knowing my staunch support for the town I had come to love would carry me to a political victory. Or, in retrospect, perhaps he threw my name in, knowing that I would win, and that it would help bring me out of my doldrums. Just a few weeks prior, my beloved wife, Mary, had died in childbirth giving life to a daughter, Bessie. Bessie herself died shortly after.

In either case, Parsons was right. The final count of the votes revealed Shaffer, 165 votes, Clum, 532. As the new mayor, I was became the head of the newly formed Citizen's Safety Committee, also known as the city Vigilance Committee, a group of business and professional men dedicated to supporting the local law enforcement whenever the need arose.

Those were heady days indeed for Tombstone. While I tried to deal with my grief over my recent loss, gas lights went up on Tombstone's main streets, the city was connected with Yuma via telegraph, and the new county of Cochise was born with Tombstone as the county seat and Johnny Behan as the first county Sheriff.

But what looked like good fortune for Behan turned out to be a point of contention between Behan and Wyatt Earp, both of whom wanted the job of County Sheriff. According to Earp, Behan double-crossed him, a spark that would smolder until the day the Earps left town.

Tombstone was a wide-open town during those times - never a dull moment. In January, a Charleston card-sharp, Johnny-Behind-The Deuce got into some trouble and shot an innocent man in Charleston; just a few miles from Tombstone. A crowd gathered and wanted to lynch Johnny right on the spot. The Charleston Constable, a man named McKelvey, brought the card-player to Tombstone for safe-keeping. But the crowd followed McKelvey and began to gather in front of the city jail. The stories of several people make the next few minutes unclear but several law-men including Wyatt Earp, Virgil Earp, and Johnny Behan fended off the crowd until the prisoner could be spirited off to Tucson under the cover of darkness.

Almost every day, or so it seemed, someone was shooting at someone else over cards, gambling, money or women. But all those events pale compared to what has been called Tombstone's defining moment.

It was about mid-day, October 26, 1881. I needed a feature story for the Epitaph and, I needed lunch. So, I went across Fremont and started up Fourth to Allen Street looking for a story and lunch. I didn't have to go far before I ran across Ike Clanton, one of the cow-boy clan, walking about carrying a rifle looking for the Earps. I said hello to him or made some sort of greeting. His reply was terse, giving some disparaging remarks about the Earps and Holliday. A moment later, City Marshal V.W. Earp appeared, disarmed Ike by buffaloing him, (it was illegal at the time to carry a firearm in Tombstone city limits) and began to drag him off to Judge Wallace's court. A moment later, Virgil's brother, Wyatt, appeared and helped his brother.

I followed along thinking this would be the story I was looking for. Although there were some tense words exchanged between Wyatt, his other brother Morgan, and Ike Clanton, the hearing, unfortunately for me was uneventful. Ike was fined a few dollars and Marshal Earp took Ike's guns for safe-keeping at one of the hotels.

But outside the courtroom, Tom McLaury, another of the cow-boy clan met the emerging Earps. (Word traveled very quickly in Tombstone when things were up.) McLaury and Wyatt exchanged some cross words. I did not hear it all, wanting to be safe distance in the event that lead should start flying. This lasted only a moment or two. Then, Wyatt slapped McLaury and drew his pistol almost simultaneously. I could see the hate instantly well up in McLaury's eyes. I suppose Wyatt could see it too because in the next instant he buffaloed McLaury with his big revolver bringing the hapless cow-boy to his knees.

Well, I figured I had my story; and my headline: "Ike Clanton Arrested By V.W. Earp - McLaury Also Subdued" I went about my way, had lunch, and returned to the Epitaph office to write up the story.

I had just finished the story at about 2:30 in the afternoon when I stood up from my desk to look out the window. I noticed the three Earp brothers and Holliday walking west on Fremont. All appeared to be quite stern and determined. Holliday wore a badge.

Just after they passed my office I saw Cochise County Sheriff Johnny Behan approach the men and try to talk to them. The Earps and Holliday didn't even slow down and pushed Behan aside as they walked. I could tell something was up and stepped outside my office door to get a better look at where they were headed.

The four stopped at the mouth of the alley between C.S. Fly's Photo Studio and Harwood's Boarding House on the back-side of the OK Corral where they spread themselves out four abreast. I could tell they were talking to some other party although I couldn't tell whom from my vantage point. I thought I should go across the street to see what was happening; maybe there would be another story in it for the paper.

It was at that point that the lead started flying. Not being heeled myself, nor knowing who the combatants were, or what the issue was, I thought it best to take cover, at least for the moment and ducked back into my office. I could hear the roar of the heavy revolvers and several shot-gun blasts. The sound of singing lead was everywhere. It was as if hell itself was paying a visit to Tombstone. Then, seconds later, it stopped.

Warily, I emerged from my hiding place and onto Fremont Street, as did many others. The smoke was still clearing as I cautiously approached the alley. Frank and Tom McLaury and Billy Clanton appeared to be dead, or mortally wounded. Holliday and brothers Morgan and Virgil were both wounded. Only Wyatt, miraculously, was untouched! Upon interviewing a few people, it became apparent that Ike Clanton had been present at the start of the affray but had run off.

I returned to my office, and rewrote the story for the next day's publication with the headline: "Yesterday's Tragedy - Three Men Hurled Into Eternity In The Duration Of A Moment". But that was only the start of things.

Over the next month or so, an inquiry was held in Judge Spicer's courtroom to determine if the Earps were guilty of murder, or had been upholding the law. Emotions ran high in town during this period. Each day, I would go to the courtroom, record the events, and write my story.

In the end, the Earps and Holliday were exonerated, but in retrospect, it seemed a Pyric Victory, not only for the Earps, but for their supporters as well. An assassination attempt was made on Virgil's life in December that year and Morg was gunned down in Campbell and Hatch's Saloon in March of '82.

As for myself, as an Earp supporter, I knew my fate was sealed. Despite the Judge's ruling, public sentiment turned against the Earps. Many thought they were the perpetrators of one of the most violent days in that camp. Of the two factions, the Earps and cow-boys, people figured that putting up with the cow-boy's rowdiness was a lesser sin, than living with out and out bloodshed brought about by the on-going feud.

But the feud did not end there, In fact, it got worse in some respects. There were many threats made upon my life and lives of those associated with the legal defense of the Earps and Holliday including Attorney Tom Fitch. I knew my political future in Tombstone was destroyed and did not run for a second term as Mayor.

In the aftermath of this whole affair, it became more and more difficult to secure advertising customers to support my paper. I decided, it was time to move on and on May 1, 1882, two years to the day after the Tombstone Epitaph was born, it was sold to Sam Purdy.

It was also about this time that I was removed as Postmaster for Tombstone. It seemed that the Earp - cow-boy incident had farther reaching influence as it appeared I had made some enemies in Washington over the affair. With my wife and child gone, and my professional and political career in jeopardy, I felt it best to try to make a new start in another place. I packed my belongings and moved to Washington D.C. to seek another job with the Postal Department.

It seemed that things were turning bad for Tombstone as well. Water was leaking into many of the mine-shafts and it became more and more difficult to work several of the mines. I left Tombstone in June of '82.

Again, I had a desk job. Although it was steady it lacked the excitement of Tombstone and certainly the challenge of San Carlos. I had spent so much time in the west, colleagues began to refer to me as Colonel, an honorary title given to those who have spent considerable time on the frontier. Although I enjoyed the recognition, I longed for actually being in the west; not just talking about it.

But Washington did have an up-side. In February, 1883, I wed Belle Atwood and things began to look up again. In December of that same year, Belle gave birth to a daughter, Caro.

And then, an opportunity hit. In February of '85, I was re-assigned to Tombstone as the Postmaster and again headed west. Tombstone was enjoying a rejuvenation with large pumps being brought in to remove water from the mines.

Although it was not the same place as it was back in '80 and '81, it was certainly a more peaceful place. Old friend, Nellie Cashman had returned to again open the Russ House with fine food for the community. Sadly, poor Judge Spicer had apparently fallen on bad times and committed suicide that year and Al Schieffelin, brother to Tombstone's found, Ed Schieffelin passed away.

Then, disaster. In May of '86 a large fire destroyed the pump house allowing the mines to fill with water. It was a devastating blow to the mining industry, a blow from which Tombstone never fully recovered. It hurt many people, put many out of work, and the citizens began to leave.

In November of '86, I decided it was time for me, along with my wife and daughter to leave as well and move on to more prosperous surroundings.

Having heard that Virgil Earp was having some measure of success as a lawman and operating a detective agency in Colton, California, we decided that was where we would go. There was a land and building boom in southern California and we headed to San Bernardino where I established Clum & O' Connor Real Estate and Insurance.

I also became a spokesperson for the San Bernardino Board Of Trade to promote the burgeoning southern California citrus industry.

All this is perhaps just as well as in May of '87, a major earthquake in Mexico opened wide the water fissures in Tombstones all but killing the mining industry and it wasn't long after that the Epitaph returned to being a weekly newspaper. At least, it was still operating and in good hands again as Reppy had recently taken it over for the second time.

And then, another adventure! Gold had been found in the far north and, just like in Tombstone, Leadville, and so many other places, the world's populace headed for what they thought was their pot-of-gold. In March of '98 I headed to Alaska to establish post offices all along that area.

I made several trips between Washington D.C. and Alaska during that period. And although Alaska was a place so far removed from anyplace I had ever been, at times, it felt like home, and old times. We met many there from the old days in Tombstone. Nellie Cashman ran a boarding house in Dawson, and still treated the miners with her usual fairness and compassion. Other old friends showed up including George Parsons. Parsons - always writing in his diary. I wonder what he ever expects to do with it?

We ran across Wyatt Earp and Sadie too. Wyatt built the first permanent structure, a wooden building, in Nome. He called it the Dexter Saloon. Wyatt made more money there than probably any miner ever dreamed of - up to $1500, per day, or so he claimed. I believe it. There was nothing else to do there but mine, and drink.

By 1908, the Klondike/Yukon gold rush was over and I returned to the states from Fairbanks that June.

In April, 1911, I retired from the Postal Service and took yet another job for the Southern Pacific railroad promoting tourism to the west, using the Southern Pacific line as a means of getting to the desert areas. People could now travel from New York to Los Angeles in a matter of days, not the weeks that it took on my first trip west.

I was enjoying life, traveling about and doing something that I developed somewhat of a flair for, speaking in front of people. But it all came to an abrupt halt when in September, 1912, I lost my beloved Belle.

I continued the job a while longer but felt a deep sense of loneliness without Belle.

Then, in October of 1914, I married Florence Baker. Although several years my junior we shared a love of many of the same things and we got along fabulously. It was Florence that convinced me that it was time to take things easier and in 1915, I left my job with the railroad and took up date farming in the Cochella Valley in California.

We had a small ranch in San Dimas for a while and about a year ago, purchased this place here in Los Angeles. Oddly enough, Los Angeles felt like being in Tombstone again as I would run into Wyatt and Sadie quite frequently. Now, with Wyatt gone, it truly feels like times have changed.

Perhaps, at some point, I should expand on these notes and write my autobiography. But, would anyone read it? Would anyone care about an Indian Agent, newspaper man, real-estate salesman and citrus-industry and tourism promoter?

Those are questions for another day, another time.

The above account contains correct dates and events but, for the purpose of this book, is somewhat fictionalized. However, in his later years, John Clum wrote a complete autobiography that was edited by his son, Woodworth, and first published in 1936.

How Could He Go Wrong

Many history buffs are familiar with Virgil Earp, brother of Wyatt and Morgan Earp of Tombstone fame. But not everyone knows there was a second Virgil Earp whose claim to fame lies not in gun slinging or faro dealing but in the spanning of two centuries - the culture of the old west and the TV game shows of the fifties.

In September of 1865, Newton Earp, older half brother to Wyatt, Virgil and Morgan Earp, married Nancy Jane Adams at Philadelphia , Missouri and settled in Lamar, Missouri. That marriage produced five children. The youngest, referred to by some sources as Virgil Edwin and other sources (Chaffin) as simply Edwin was born either April 19, 1880 in Tombstone Arizona. (Earp Files) or 1879 in Kansas (Chaffin).

Virgil came to know his uncles and family legacy in that town very well; the OK Corral shootout happening only 18 months after his birth. For a time, Virgil lived the classic "western" lifestyle, carrying a six-shooter at sixteen and serving as Sheriff of Paradise Valley, Nevada at eighteen. He claims to have killed three men by the time he was 21, the first being a man who was molesting his sister.

In 1903 at age 24, he claims to have joined his Uncle Wyatt on a trip to Mexico to track down Pete Spence and Indian Charlie, two men Wyatt held responsible for the assassination of his brother Morgan - an act of retaliation for the OK Corral shooting. Virgil claimed to have killed Indian Charlie while Wyatt exacted revenge on Pete Spence. (Other records indicate that Wyatt himself shot and killed Pete Spence in March 1882, in Tucson. The same records also show that approximately one month later, Indian Charlie met the same fate at the hands of Wyatt Earp, just outside Tombstone. It is also commonly known that in 1903, Wyatt and his wife Josephine were traveling throughout the California desert on prospecting expeditions, spending considerable time in a little town on the California/Nevada border which now bears his name; Earp, California.

At any rate, Virgil was certainly fully familiar with western lore and legend. Information which served him well when, in 1958, he appeared on the television quiz show, "The $64,000 Question" and won $32,000 in the "Wild West" category! He maintained that a woman of those days in the "Wild West" was actually safer then than at present. (1958) He was noted as saying, "In the old days there was no such thing as juvenile delinquency, no house robberies and no organized government. There was just good men and bad men - and one policy, a life for a life".

A short time after his TV appearance, and amid the furor of the government's investigation into "rigged" TV game shows, Virgil was asked if he had been coached in any way regarding his answers. He replied with a flat "No! - Who could tell *me* anything about the west"!

Virgil Edwin Earp died on November 20, 1959. An Associated Press obituary for him is titled, "Last Fighting Earp Dies Peacefully Of Old Age".

Information from the Earp Files of the Colton Public Library, Colton, CA

Who Is Buried In Morgan Earp's Grave?

Who is buried in Morgan Earp's grave? Is it really Morgan; brother to famous lawmen Wyatt and Virgil Earp? Or is it some long forgotten, unidentified hapless soul? How could such an icon of the West; a hero of lore and life meet such an unceremonious end leaving his grave's occupant suspect? The facts surrounding Morgan's death are clear and documented. The facts about his burial are not.

The series of events that would end Morgan Earp's life began when he joined his brothers Wyatt and Virgil as a Deputy Sheriff in the wild mining town of Tombstone, Arizona Territory. The Earps were not only lawmen but businessmen with interests in mining, gambling and the politics of a prosperous growing community. The Clanton-McLaury faction passed themselves off as ranchers but their main concerns were cattle rustling, drinking and getting into trouble. The Earps and the Clantons were at opposite ends of both social and political spectrums.

The friction between the Earps and the Clanton-McLaury gang came to a boil on October 26, 1881. Ike and Billy Clanton joined by Frank and Tom McLaury and Billy Claiborne were in Tombstone, brazenly carrying their six-shooters in defiance of Tombstone's gun law, making menacing remarks and threatening the Earp's lives. Compelled to enforce the law, and joined by their compatriot "Doc" Holliday, Virgil, Wyatt and Morgan met their foes in an alley off Fremont Street, meaning only to disarm them. But the gang would not be disarmed and the bullets started to fly. It would become the most famous 30 seconds in western history, the most famous gun battle of all time; the gunfight at the OK Corral. When the smoke cleared, Frank and Tom McLaury and Billy Clanton were dead. Billy Claiborne and Ike Clanton had run off. Wyatt was unscathed. Doc suffered only a superficial wound while Virgil suffered a leg wound but would survive. Morgan's shoulder wound would heal but his fate was sealed. The Clanton's cowboy pride was too severely damaged to let the incident go without revenge.

Virgil was the first to taste the fury of the Clanton's vengeance. Just before midnight on December 28, 1881, Virgil stepped from the Oriental Saloon and crossed Fifth Street.   Five shot gun blasts rang out. Three went wild. The fourth tore a gaping hole in Virgil's left side and the fourth nearly severed his left arm. Virgil would survive and later became the first Sheriff of Colton, California.

Then, it was Morgan's turn. The town of Tombstone would live up to it's name once again. On the evening of March 17, 1882 Morgan was enjoying a game of billiards with Bob Hatch, the owner of an Allen Street billiard hall which was a favorite roost for the Earps. Hatch leaned over the table, about to make a shot. Morgan stood with his back to the rear door of the pool hall chalking his cue while Wyatt sat in a chair propped against a wall looking on. It was approximately 11:30 PM. Four members of the Clanton gang, Pete Spence, Frank Stilwell, Florentino Cruz and Hank Swilling approached the rear pool hall door. The glass panes in the rear door shattered to the floor as Clanton guns roared and the air filled with lead. One slug whizzed over Wyatt's head and buried itself into the wall. Morgan was not so lucky. A bullet caught him square in the back, severing his spine. He died an hour later.

Details about what happened to Morgan Earp after the Tombstone shooting are somewhat sketchy. It is commonly thought that Wyatt stayed in Tombstone while Virgil returned to the Earp family home in Colton California to see to Morgan's burial. Other accounts have another Earp brother, James, accompanying Morgan's body. Some say Wyatt returned withy his brother's body. Some historians dispute the thought that any of the Earps ever returned to

Colton. Yet in a newspaper article from 1959, a Mrs. Estelle Miller, granddaughter to Nicholas Earp and daughter to Mrs. Adell Edwards, only sister of the Earp brothers stated that it was Wyatt who brought Morgan's body back to Colton. She also stated that she was not sure what cemetery Morgan had been buried in. At the time there were two cemeteries in Colton, the Agua Mansa, reported to be used chiefly by Colton's earliest settlers from New Mexico and those of Mexican descent, and the Mt. Slover cemetery. It is generally assumed that Morgan was buried in the Mt. Slover cemetery. Reports indicate that the grave was originally marked with a headstone but vandals or souvenir seekers either destroyed it or carried it away. For reasons unknown, the marker was never replaced.

But even in death, Morgan would not be able to rest! He would have to make one last journey! During the 1880's, Colton, California was growing as a center of commerce. As Colton grew, so did the need for more railroad lines and the space to lay track. Part of the land occupied by the Mt. Slover cemetery was sold to the railroad. On November 29, 1892, 16 bodily remains were exhumed from the Mt. Slover cemetery and re-interred in the Hermosa Cemetery a few miles away. Records show an H.L. Watson, a G.W. Dent, a Henry Anderson, a Dennis McAuliff, an unknown Young Lady and 11 other "Unknowns" were exhumed and re-interred that November day. The only other identification given to the "Unknowns" were, "wore gray coat and blue pants" and "had shoes on". It is generally assumed that one of the "Unknowns" was the body of Morgan Earp.

Efforts to locate the original Mt. Slover cemetery or find any traces of what might have been Morgan's original grave have proven hopeless. About 1896, a cement company purchased what was possibly the remaining original cemetery land and began quarrying the stone from Mt. Slover to make cement. The company is still there today. Any traces of the cemetery have either been built upon or bulldozed over.

It was not enough that Morgan Earp endured years of anonymity without a grave marker; indignity would follow Morgan once again! Buried for a second time, his grave, or perhaps it should be said, his alleged grave, was left unmarked and stayed that way for almost 100 years. Then, in 1991, in true western fashion, a "posse" of US Marshals came to the rescue.

Steve Herrea, Jim Real and Carol Grey all have four things in common. They are members of the Southern California Paraders Association, a ceremonial equine marching unit. They are all members of the United States Marshal's Posse; a group whose purpose is to represent the US Marshal Service in ceremonial events such as parades. They all share an interest in western history in general and the Earps in particular and they all agreed that a man who died in a town called Tombstone should not spend eternity without a tombstone of his own. It is a combination of interests that led to extensive research into Morgan Earp's interment and the eventual placement, on March 16, 1991, of a tombstone on the site where Morgan is *believed* to be buried. Paid for with funds from the Paraders Association, the gravestone epitaph reads, "US Deputy Marshal, Morgan S. Earp, Born 1851, Assassinated, Tombstone Arizona, March 18, 1882" Finally, after so many years, a fitting tribute was paid to one of western history's most famous legends.

But is it really Morgan Earp who lies in the grave at Colton's Hermosa Cemetery? We of the living will never know. But maybe Morgan will rest easier now that his 100 years of anonymity are over.

Hamburgers and Gunslingers

It is the early 1890's, the start of the last decade of the 19th century. According to the 1890 US Census, the western frontier is closed. But is it… really?

On many reservations, Indians are performing the Ghost Dance scaring the daylights out of hardened military men, afraid that the superstitious Indians will actually be able to resurrect their dead ancestors and overcome the US Army in one last bloody battle, reminiscent of Custer's last battle in 1876. The Army even goes so far as to provide arms for the citizenry to defend themselves in a total Indian uprising.

Cripple Creek, Colorado is one of the newest boomtown overflowing with miners, businessmen, saloon keepers, soiled doves, card sharps, and all the trappings of a mining town.

In Coffeeville, Kansas, the Dalton gang tries unsuccessfully to rob two banks at once. The local citizens, wise to their ridiculous false-beard disguises arm themselves and cut down the gang in hail of lead!

Sioux Indians attack a wagon train on the site of the Wounded Knee massacre of several years before. It seems that little has changed from the days of the first settlers back in '49.

Or has it…?

While Indians danced, stages and banks were robbed, "sporting men" cheated miners, and gold and silver were dug from the ground west of the Mississippi, the 1893 World's Columbian Exposition opened in Chicago. In retrospect, the Exposition seemed to be a bridge linking the end of the 19th century, and the beginning of the 20th. It places a bookmark in time, the prior pages being concerned with the time between the Lewis and Clark Expedition, and the end of the careers of those like Bill Miner and Butch and Sundance.

In March 1890, Senator Daniel of Virginia introduced a bill to authorize an exposition to celebrate the 400th anniversary of the discovery of America by Christopher Columbus.   The act was entitled: *An act to provide for celebrating the 400th anniversary of the discovery of America by Christopher Columbus, by holding an international exhibition of arts, industries, manufactures, and the products of the soil, mine, and sea, in the city of Chicago, in the State of Illinois.*

But it would be much more than the celebration of a 400-year-old mariner. In fact, it seems that the memory of ol' Chris Columbus was lost in what was then the Disney World of the 19th century.

As soon as work began on what would eventually cover over 600 acres of exhibits, the crowds began to gather and watch as ornate building after ornate building was erected. In fact, the construction itself became such an attraction that the World's Columbian Commission began charging fare admittance of .25 to watch the construction!

Steam plants were built at a cost of over $1 million generating over 24,000-horse power (imagine a stage coach pulled by that many horses!) used to generate electricity for the Exposition. This was three times the electrical consumption of the entire city of Chicago.

The Exposition must have resembled, at that time, the Las Vegas strip of today. There were 93,000 incandescent lights, 5,000 arc lights, and a multitude of electrically operated machinery. The Exposition also sported the world's first electrically operated elevated railway and an electrically operated moving sidewalk. (Ed. Note: I'll think about that every time I go through an airport!)

The site also had two gigantic water treatment plants to take care of the all the sewage and waste created by an attraction that would be visited by over 27 million people. The pumping stations were open for the public to see as a sort of "Welcome To Hydraulic Technology" exhibit. Such a huge capacity was needed to accommodate the 6,500 lavatories and toilets. Chicago was no place for an "out-house".

On October 26, 1892, only 11 years to the day after that fateful incident in Tombstone. Vice President Levi Morton dedicated the site of the Exposition and on May 1, 1893, President Grover Cleveland opened the fair.

And then, the people came… in droves, from the east, the west, and from all over the globe as many countries were represented at the colossal event! In fact, on one day, October 9, 1893 (Chicago Day) over 700,000 people went through the gate.

By 1893, the world was growing smaller. It now took only 26 hours to go from New York to Chicago, and a little over 3 days from San Francisco to Chicago. If you were outside the US, say in Russia, it would have taken 16 days to get to Chicago, 11 days from Austria, 10 days from Scotland and 9 days from London.

General admission to the fair was .50 for adults, .25 for children and kids under 6 were free. Many exhibits charged an additional fee of from .25 to .75 per admission. Private cameras were allowed on the site for an additional $2 per day.

Interestingly enough, many of the same products that we enjoy today were introduced at the fair. In fact, many of the products won awards during the fair for their ingenuity and unique-ness. The products used that award-winning moniker in their advertising for months afterward. Some of the more significant of these products were:

- The first commemorative stamp set
- The first commemorative coin set
- The first picture post cards
- Cracker Jack candy
- Aunt Jemima Syrup
- Cream Of Wheat cereal
- Shredded Wheat
- Pabst Beer
- Juicy Fruit gum
- Gray's Teleautograph (a device the could reproduce handwriting at a distance; sort of the forerunner to the fax machine)
- Kinetograph (Thomas Edison's precursor to the movie projector.)

Consider the significance that these products, available today, have in joining the world of the old west, and the 19th century with everyday life today! Perhaps even more significant, only because of their pervasiveness in everyday global society was the introduction during the fair of the hamburger and diet carbonated soda! Wyatt Earp, and many of the Tombstone gang still living at that time were one step away from McDonald's!

Another concept introduced at the fair, and that exists today, is the carnival concept and the mid-way. While trying to take a high-brow approach to the celebration of the founder of a country, the Fair Commission unwittingly started something that today, has, perhaps, less than a sterling connotation but is nonetheless, purely American!

And what "carnival" would be complete without a Ferris wheel. The Exposition had a Ferris wheel. In fact, they had the first Ferris wheel created by George Ferris himself. The ride would take visitors over 200 feet above the fair grounds for two full revolutions!

But certainly more significant than the seminal beginnings of what have become some of the trappings of current pop-culture, was the fact that industry – big industry, and politics were coming together to conduct what would evolve into a marriage of nation-wide, then world-wide business.

It was at this fair, in July, 1894, that Frederick Jackson Turner, a former newspaper editor, College Professor and Doctor of History addressed the American Historical Association in a speech entitled, "The Significance Of The Frontier In American History". In it, he espoused the importance of understanding the importance of frontier ideology and its pervasiveness in the then present-day American culture. He discussed not only the simple movement of people from the Atlantic to the Pacific Ocean, but also how culture changed to adapt to varying environments and the effect of these changing environs on the aggregate social culture of as country.

Turner noted that the first settlers in America stood on the "doorstep" of a new land and the "western frontier" lay at the end of their toes on east-coast beaches. Gradually, the "western frontier" moved to the Allegheny Mountains, the Mississippi River, the Great Plains, the Rocky Mountains, and eventually, the Pacific Ocean. Those first settlers brought with them the culture and conventions of Europe and through incremental changes, made the slightly revised culture work in the "New Land" in what eventually became settled and "hospitable" property.

Eventually, the urge to move forced people ever-westward in a constant progression of having to leave a civilized society for uncivilized environs. This, together with the simple passage of time, and technological changes and circumstances forced yet more incremental cultural changes. It was Turner's thesis that the constant succession of frontiers, and constant societal changes precipitated by those frontiers, led to what has become and change from a European society to one that is truly American. And with the "closing of the frontier" as stated in the 1890 US census, America would now have to deal with the fact that they could no longer "escape" to a new frontier and a new beginning; that American would now have to deal with living within a confined space and technology and other cultural changes would be the "new frontier".

In his own time, Turner's address seemed trivial. Even his own parents, visiting the fair, did not attend the lecture. Yet, in retrospect, and in view of the time period in which he lived and the time and place where his address was given, his words are extremely succinct in understanding the old west and it's place in American History. Reading his words today help us to understand how the ever-moving frontier helped shape the character of the American people and the nature of America's institutions.

Despite the spectacle of the Exposition, its majesty would be plagued by fire. On July 10, 1893 a major fire destroyed one of the main buildings killing 17 people. The fair closed on October 26, 1893 but that would not stop the continued bad luck at the site. Another major fire in January, 1894 destroyed four more main buildings and yet another fire in July of that year burned seven more.

Yet, despite the fires and other problems, the 1893 World's Columbian Exposition remains even today as a milepost in the history of the United States, and the platform upon which one man, Frederick Jackson Turner, unwittingly, had a lasting impact on the old west.

Frederick Jackson Turner: The Unappreciated Orator

"The true point of view in the history of this nation is not the Atlantic coast, it is the Great West" so said Frederick Jackson Turner as he addressed the American Historical Association during the 1893 World's Columbian Exposition in Chicago.

At the time, the speech seemed trivial and unimportant to his peers. Even his own parents, visiting the fair did not attend his speech. Fortunately, the speech has managed to survive time and in looking at it in the context of modern times, and knowing that this was written prior to 1900, Turner's words are quite profound.

Of course, Turner never had a thing to do with Tombstone in particular; so one may ask what his words are doing in a book about that famous mining camp? Well, if you are reading this book, you likely not only enjoy tales of Tombstone, but also of the old west and American history in general. And Turner provides a fascinating perspective on American expansionism and how it influenced his world in 1893, and how it continues to affect our world here in the 21st century.

Frederick Turner was born on November 14, 1861 in Wisconsin to a family who can be traced directly back to English Puritans. He attended the University of Wisconsin graduating in 1884 working in the newspaper world until he became a university instructor in oratory at his alma mater.

While working, he also attended classes earning his Masters Of Arts in History at Wisconsin and went on to receive his doctorate of History at Johns Hopkins University. He went back to the University of Wisconsin as an Assistant professor of History in 1889.

It was about this timer that he began working on his thesis which noted that past historians had not given ample analysis of the westward expansion of America, looking primarily at dates and places and leaving aside the social impact not only of the total push from Atlantic to Pacific, but how each individual advancement affected people (especially the Native Americans) and how they evolved socially, culturally, intellectually, and morally.

Upon noting that only three years before, the US government had declared the frontier closed, Turner pondered the proposition that after 270 years of constant expansion, and always knowing on a conscious and cultural scale that the land would spread out endlessly, that expansion had finally come to an end. And now, Americans would have to accept, for the very first time, that they were within a confined area, if they wanted to stay within the confines of the continent.

This theory is significant in the context of this book, noting that time and circumstance brought many of the same people together from the east coast to Tucson, Prescott, Tombstone, and eventually to the Klondike region, all looking for the same thing – that elusive pot of gold.

People like Butch and Sundance, Ben Kilpatrick and Bill Miner had to know about this time, if not consciously, at least institutively, that their days of "riding off into the sunset" and anonymity, away from pursuing lawmen were numbered. Here then, is the text of Mr. Turner's speech, as it was given in 1893.

The Significance Of The Frontier In American History

By Frederick Jackson Turner 1893

In a recent bulletin of the Superintendent of the Census for 1890 appear these significant words: Up to and including 1880 the country had a frontier of settlement, but at present the unsettled area has been so broken into by isolated bodies of settlement that there can hardly be said to be a frontier line. In the discussion of its extent, its westward movement, etc., it can not, therefore, any longer have a place in the census reports." This brief official statement marks the closing of a great historic movement. Up to our own day American history has been in a large degree the history of the colonization of the Great West. The existence of an area of free land, its continuous recession, and the advance of American settlement westward, explain American development.

Behind institutions, behind constitutional forms and modifications, lie the vital forces that call these organs into life and shape them to meet changing conditions. The peculiarity of American institutions is the fact that they have been compelled to adapt themselves to the changes of an expanding people-to the changes involved in crossing a continent, in winning a wilderness, and in developing at each area of this progress out of the primitive economic and political conditions of the frontier into the complexity of city life. Said Calhoun in 1817, "'We are great, and rapidly ---I was about to say fearfully ---growing!" So saying, he touched the distinguishing feature of American life. All peoples show development; the germ theory of politics has been sufficiently emphasized. In the case of most nations, however, the development has occurred in a limited area, and if the nation has expanded, it has met other growing peoples whom it has conquered. But in the case of the United States we have a different phenomenon. Limiting our attention to the Atlantic coast,we have the familiar phenomenon of the evolution of institutions in a limited area, such as the rise of representative government the differentiation of simple colonial governments into complex organs; the progress from primitive industrial society, without division of labor, up to manufacturing civilization. But we have in addition to this a recurrence of the process of volution in each western area reached in the process of expansion. Thus American development has exhibited not merely advance along a single line, but a return to primitive conditions on a continually advancing frontier line, and a new development for that area. American social development has been continually beginning over again on the frontier. This perennial, this fluidity of American life, this expansion westward-with its few opportunities, its continuous touch with the simplicity of primitive society, furnish the forces dominating American character. The true point of view in the history of this nation is not the Atlantic coast, it i5 the Great West. Even the slavery struggle, which is made so exclusive an object of attention by writers like Professor von Holst, occupies its important place in American history because of its relation to westward expansion.

In this advance, the frontier is the outer edge of the wave the meeting point between savagery and civilization. Much has been written about the frontier from the point of view of border warfare and the chase, but as a field for the serious study of the economist and the historian it has been neglected.

The American frontier is sharply distinguished from the European frontier ---a fortified boundary line running through dense populations. The most significant thing about the American frontier is that it lies at the hither edge of free land. In the census reports it is treated as the margin of that settlement which has a density of two or more to the square mile. The term is an elastic one, and for our purposes does not need sharp definition. We shall consider the whole frontier belt, including the Indian country and the outer margin of the "settled area" of the census reports. This paper will make no attempt to treat the subject exhaustively; its aim is simply to call attention to the frontier as a fertile field for investigation, and to suggest some of the problems which arise in connection with it.

In the settlement of America we have to observe how European life entered the continent, and how America modified and developed that life and reacted on Europe. Our early history is the study of European germs developing in an American environment. Too exclusive attention has been paid by institutional students to the Germanic origins, too little to the American factors the frontier is the line of most rapid and effective Americanization. After wilderness masters the colonist finds him a European in dress, industries, tools, modes of travel, and thought. It takes him from the railroad car and puts him in the birch canoe. It strips off the garments of civilization and arrays him in the hunting shirt and the moccasin. It puts him in the log cabin of the Cherokee and Iroquois and runs an Indian palisade around him. Before long he has gone to planting Indian corn and plowing with a sharp stick; he shouts the war cry and takes the scalp in orthodox Indian fashion. In short, at the frontier the environment is at first too strong for the man. He must accept the conditions which it furnishes, or perish, and so he fits himself into the Indian clearings and follows the Indian trails. Little by little he transforms the wilderness, but the outcome is not the old Europe, not simply the development of Germanic germs, any more than the first phenomenon was a case of reversion to the Germanic mark. The fact is that here is a new product that is American. At first, the frontier was the Atlantic coast the frontier of Europe in a very real sense. Moving westward, the frontier became more and more American. As successive terminal moraines result from successive glaciations, so each frontier leaves its traces behind it, and when it becomes a settled area the region still partakes of the frontier characteristics. Thus the advance of the frontier has meant a steady movement away from the influence of Europe, a steady growth of independence on American lines. And to study this advance, the men who grew up under these conditions, and the political, economic, and social results of it, is to study the really American part of our history.

In the course of the seventeenth century the frontier was advanced up the Atlantic river courses, just beyond the "fall line," and the tidewater region became the settled area. In the first half of the eighteenth century another advance occurred. Traders followed the Delaware and Shawnee Indians to the Ohio as early as the end of the first quarter of the century. Governor Spotswood, of Virginia, made an expedition in 1714 across the Blue Ridge. The end of the first quarter of the century saw the advance of the Scotch-Irish and the Palatine Germans up the Shenandoah Valley into the western part of Virginia, and along the Piedmont region of the Carolinas. The Germans in New York pushed the frontier of settlement up the Mohawk to German Flats. In Pennsylvania the town of Bedford indicates the line of settlement. Settlements had begun on New Rivers a branch of the Kanawhan and on the sources of the Yadkin and French Broad. The King attempted to arrest the advance by his proclamation of 1763, forbidding settlement beyond the sources of the rivers flowing into the Atlantic; but in vain. In the period of the Revolution the frontier crossed the Alleghenies into Kentucky and Tennessee, and the upper waters of the Ohio were settled. When the first census was taken in 1790, the continuous settled area was bounded by a line which ran near the coast of Maine, and included New England except a portion of Vermont and New Hampshire, New York along the Hudson and up the Mohawk about Schenectady, eastern and southern Pennsylvania, Virginia well across the Shenandoah Valley, and the Carolinas and eastern Georgia. Beyond this region of continuous settlement were the small settled areas of Kentucky and Tennessee, and the Ohio, with the mountains intervening between them and the Atlantic area, thus giving a new and important character to the frontier. The isolation of the region increased its peculiarly American, and the need of transportation facilities to connect it with the East called out important schemes of internal improvement, which will be noted farther on. The "West," as a self-conscious section, began to evolve.

From decade to decade distinct advances of the frontier occurred. By the census of 1820 the settled area included Ohio, southern Indiana and Illinois, southeastern Missouri, and about one-half of Louisiana. This settled area had surrounded Indian areas, and the management of these tribes became an object of political concern.

The frontier region of the time lay along the Great Lakes, where Astor's American Fur Company operated in the Indian trade, and beyond the Mississippi, where Indian traders extended their activity even to the Rocky Mountains; Florida also furnished frontier conditions. The Mississippi River region was the scene of typical frontier settlements.

The rising steam navigation on western waters, the opening of the Erie Canal, and the westward extension of cotton culture added five frontier states to the Union in this period. Grund, writing in 1836, declares: "'It appears then that the universal disposition of Americans to emigrate to the western wilderness, in order to enlarge their dominion over inanimate nature, is the actual result of an expansive power which is inherent in them, and which by continually agitating all classes of society is constantly throwing a large portion of the whole population on the extreme confines of the State, in order to gain space for its development. Hardly is a new State or Territory formed before the same principle manifests itself again and gives rise to a further emigration; and so is it destined to go on until a physical barrier must finally obstruct its progress."

In the middle of this century the line indicated by the present eastern boundary of Indian Territory, Nebraska, and Kansas marked the frontier of the Indian country. Minnesota and Wisconsin still exhibited frontier conditions, but the distinctive frontier of the period is found in California, where the gold discoveries had sent a sudden tide of adventurous miners, and in Oregon, and the settlements in Utah. As the frontier had leaped over the Alleghenies, so now it skipped the Great Plains and the Rocky Mountains; and in the same way that the advance of the frontiersman beyond the Alleghenies had caused the rise of important questions of transportation and internal improvement, so now the settlers beyond the Rocky Mountains needed means of communication with the East, and in the furnishing of these arose the settlement of the Great Plains and the development of still another kind of frontier life. Railroads, fostered by land grants, sent an increasing tide of immigrants into the Far West. The United States Army fought a series of Indian wars in Minnesota, Dakota, and the Indian Territory.

By 1880 the settled area had been pushed into northern Michigan, Wisconsin, and Minnesota, along Dakota rivers, and in the Black Hills region, and was ascending the rivers of Kansas and Nebraska. The development of mines in Colorado had drawn isolated frontier settlements into that region, and Montana and Idaho were receiving settlers. The frontier was found in these mining camps and the ranches of the Great Plains. The superintendent of the census for 1890 reports, as previously stated, that the settlements of the West lie so scattered over the region that there can no longer be said to be a frontier line.

In these successive frontiers we find natural boundary lines which have served to mark and to affect the characteristics of the frontiers, namely: the "fall line"; the Allegheny Mountains; the Mississippi the Missouri where its direction approximates north and south; the line of the arid lands, approximately the ninety-ninth meridian; and the Rocky Mountains. The fall line marked the frontier of the seventeenth century; the Alleghenies that of the eighteenth; the Mississippi that of the first quarter of the nineteenth; the Missouri that of the middle of this century (omitting the California movement); and the belt of the Rocky Mountains and the arid tract, the present frontier. Each was won by a series of Indian wars.

At the Atlantic frontier one can study the germs of processes repeated at each successive frontier. We have the complex European life sharply precipitated by the wilderness into the simplicity of primitive conditions. The first frontier had to meet its Indian question, its question of the disposition of the public domain, of the means of intercourse with older settlements, of the extension of political organization, of religious and educational activity. And the settlement of these and similar questions for one frontier served as a guide for the next. The American student needs not to go to the "prim little townships of Sleswick" for illustrations of the law of continuity and development. For example, he may study the origin of our land policies in the colonial land policy; he may see how the system grew by adapting the statutes to the customs of the successive frontiers. He may see how the mining experience in the lead regions of Wisconsin, Illinois, and Iowa was applied to the mining laws of the Sierras, and how our Indian policy has been a series of experimentations on successive frontiers. Each tier of new States has found in the older ones material for its constitutions. Each frontier has made similar contributions to American haracters, as will be discussed farther on.

But with all these similarities there are essential differences, due to the place element and the time element is evident that the farming frontier of the Mississippi Valley presents different conditions from the mining frontier of the Rocky Mountains. The frontier reached by the Pacific Railroad, surveyed into rectangles, guarded by the United States Army, and recruited by the daily immigrant ship, moves forward at a swifter pace and in a different way than the frontier reached by the birch canoe or the pack horse. The geologist traces patiently the shores of ancient seas, maps their areas, and compares the older and the newer. It would be a work worth the historian's labors to mark these various frontiers and in detail compare one with another. Not only would there result a more adequate conception of American development and characteristics, but invaluable additions would be made to the history of society.

Loria, the Italian economist, has urged the study of colonial life as an aid in understanding the stages of European development, affirming that colonial settlement is for economic science what the mountain is for geology, bringing to light primitive stratifications. "America," he says, "has the key to the historical enigma which Europe has sought for centuries in vain, and the land which has no history reveals luminously the course of universal history." There is much truth in this. The United States lies like a huge page in the history of society. Line by line as we read this continental page from West to East we find the record of social evolution. It begins with the Indian and the hunter; it goes on to tell of the disintegration of savagery by the entrance of the trader, the pathfinder of civilization; we read the annals of the pastoral stage in ranch life; the exploitation of the soil by the raising of unrotated crops of corn and wheat in sparsely settled farming communities; the intensive culture of the denser farm settlement; and finally the manufacturing organization with city and factory system. This page is familiar to the student of census statistics, but how little of it has been used by our historians. Particularly in eastern States this page is a palimpsest. What is now a manufacturing State was in an earlier decade an area of intensive farming. Earlier yet it had been a wheat area, and still earlier the "range" had attracted the cattle-herder. Thus Wisconsin, now developing manufacture, is a State with varied agricultural interests, But earlier it was given over to almost exclusive grain-raising, like North Dakota, at the present time.

Each of these areas has had an influence in our economic and political history; the evolution of each into a higher stage has worked political transformations. But what constitutional historian has made any adequate attempt to interpret political facts by the light of these social areas and changes?

The Atlantic frontier was compounded of fisherman, fur-trader, miner, cattle-raiser, and farmer. Excepting the fisherman, each type of industry was on the march toward the West, impelled by an irresistible attraction. Each passed in successive waves across the continent. Stand at Cumberland Gap and watch the procession of civilization, marching single file- the buffalo following the trail to the salt springs, the Indian, the fur-trader and hunter, the cattle-raiser, the pioneer farmer and the frontier has passed by. Stand at South Pass in the Rockies a century later and see the same procession with wider intervals between. The unequal rate of advance compels us to distinguish the frontier into the trader's frontier, the rancher's frontier, or the miner's frontier, and the farmer's frontier. When the mines and the cowpens were still near the fall line the traders' pack trains were tinkling across the Alleghenies, and the French on the Great Lakes were fortifying their posts, alarmed by the British trader's birch canoe. When the trappers scaled the Rockies, the farmer was still near the mouth of the Missouri.

Why was it that the Indian trader passed so rapidly across the continent? What effects followed from the trader's frontier? The trade was coeval with American discovery Norsemen, Vespucius, Verrazani, Hudson, John Smith, all trafficked for furs. The Plymouth Pilgrims settled in Indian cornfields, and their first return cargo was of beaver and lumber. The records of the various New England colonies show how steadily exploration was carried into the wilderness by this trade. What is true for New England is, as would be expected, even plainer for the rest of the colonies. All along the coast from Maine to Georgia the Indian trade opened up the river courses. Steadily the trader passed westward, utilizing the older lines of French trade. The Ohio, the Great Lakes, the Mississippi, and the Platte, the lines of western advance, were ascended by traders. They found the passes in the Rocky Mountains and guided Lewis and Clark, Fremont, and Bidwell. The explanation of the rapidity of this advance is connected with the effects of the trader on the Indian's trading post left the unarmed tribes at the mercy of those that had purchased firearms a truth which the Iroquois Indians wrote in blood, and so the remote and unvisited tribes gave eager welcome to the trade;?" The savages," wrote La Salle, "take better care of us French than of their own children; from us only can they get guns and goods. "This accounts for the trader's power and the rapidity of his advance;" Thus the disintegrating forces of civilization entered the wilderness. Every river valley and Indian trail became a fissure in Indian society, and so that society became honeycombed. Long before the pioneer farmer appeared on the scene, primitive Indian life had passed away. The farmers met Indians armed with guns. The trading frontier, while steadily undermining Indian power by making the tribes ultimately dependent on the whites, yet, through its sale of guns, gave to the Indian increased power of resistance to the farming frontier. French colonization was dominated by its trading frontier; English colonization by its farming frontier. There was an antagonism between the two frontiers as between the two nations. Said Duquesne to the Iroquois, '"Are you ignorant of the difference between the king of England and the king of France? Go see the forts that our king has established and you will see that you can still hunt under their very walls. They have been placed for your advantage in places which you frequent. The English, on the contrary, are no sooner in possession of a place than the game is driven away. The forest falls before them as they advance, and the soil is laid bare so that you can scarce find the wherewithal to erect a shelter for the night."

 And yet, in spite of this opposition of the interests of the trader and the farmer, the Indian trade pioneered the way for civilization. The buffalo trail became the Indian trail, and this became the trader's "traces'; the trails widened into roads, and the roads into turnpikes, and these in turn were transformed into railroads. The same origin can be shown for the railroads of the South, the Far West, and the Dominion of Canada. The trading posts reached by these trails were on the sites of Indian villages which had been placed in positions suggested by nature; and these trading posts, situated so as to command the water systems of the country, have grown into such cities as Albany, Pittsburgh, Detroit, Chicago, St. Louis, Council Bluffs, and Kansas City.

Thus civilization in America has followed the arteries made by geology, pouring an ever richer tide through h them, until at last the slender paths of aboriginal intercourse have been broadened and interwoven into the complex mazes of modern commercial lines; the wilderness has been interpenetrated by lines of civilization growing ever more numerous. It is like the steady growth of complex nervous system for the originally simple, inert continent. If one would understand why we are today one nation, rather than a collection of isolated states, he must study this economic and social consolidation of the country. In this progress from savage conditions lie topics for the evolutionist.

The effect of the Indian frontier as a consolidating agent in our history is important. From the close of the seventeenth century various inter-colonial congresses have been called to treat with Indians and establish common measures of defense. Particularism was strongest in colonies with no Indian frontier. This frontier stretched along the western border like a cord of union. The Indian was a common danger, demanding united action. Most celebrated of these conferences was the Albany Congress of 1754, called to treat with the Six Nations, and to consider plans of union. Even a cursory reading of the plan proposed by the congress reveals the importance of the frontier. The powers of the general council and the officers were, chiefly, the determination of peace and war with the Indians, the regulation of Indian trade, the purchase of Indian lands, and the creation and government of new settlements as a security against the Indians. It is evident that the unifying tendencies of the Revolutionary period were facilitated by the previous cooperation in the regulation of the frontier. In this connection may be mentioned
the importance of the frontier, from that day to this, as a military training school, keeping alive the power of resistance to aggression, and developing the stalwart and rugged qualities of the frontiersman.

 It would not be possible in the limits of this paper to trace the other frontiers across the continent. Travelers of the eighteenth century found the "cowpens" among the canebrakes and peavine pastures of the South, and the "cow drivers" took their droves to Charleston, Philadelphia, and New York. Travelers at the close of the War of 1812 met droves of more than a thousand cattle and swine from the interior of Ohio going to Pennsylvania to fatten for the Philadelphia market. The ranges of the Great Plains, with ranch and cowboy and nomadic life, are things of yesterday and of today. The experience of the Carolina cowpens guided the ranchers of Texas. One element favoring the rapid extension of the rancher's frontier is the fact that in a remote country lacking transportation facilities the product must be in small bulk, or must be able to transport itself, and the cattle-raiser could easily drive his product to market. The effect of these great ranches on the subsequent agrarian history of the localities in which they existed should be studied.

The maps of the census reports show an uneven advance of the farmer's frontier, with tongues of settlement pushed forward and with indentations of wilderness. In part this is due to Indian resistance, in part to the location of river valleys and passes, in part to the unequal force of the centers of frontier attraction. Among the important centers of attraction may be mentioned the following: fertile and favorably situated soils, salt springs, mines, and army posts.

The frontier army post, serving to protect the settlers from the Indians, has also acted as a wedge to open the Indian country, and has been a nucleus for settlement. in this connection mention should also be made of the government military and exploring expeditions in determining the lines of settlement. But all the more important expeditions were greatly indebted to the earliest pathmakers, the Indian guides, the traders and trappers, and the French voyageurs, who were inevitable parts of governmental expeditions from the days of Lewis and Clark. Each expedition was an epitome of the previous factors in western advance.

In an interesting monograph, Victor Hehn has traced the effect of salt upon early European development, and has pointed out how it affected the lines of settlement and the form of administration. A similar study might be made for the salt springs of the United States The early settlers were tied to the coast by the need of salt, without which they could not preserve their meats or live in comfort. Writing in 1752~ Bishop Spangenburg says of a colony for which he was seeking lands in North Carolina, "They will require salt & other necessaries which they can neither manufacture nor raise. Either they must go to Charleston, which is 300 miles distant . . . Or else they must go to Boling's Point in Va on a branch of the James & is also 300 miles from here . . . Or else they must go down the Roanoke --I know not how many miles--where salt is brought up from the Cape Fear." This may serve as a typical illustration. An annual pilgrimage to the coast for salt thus became essential. Taking flocks or furs and ginseng root, the early settlers sent their pack trains after seeding time each year to the coast. This proved to be an important educational influence, since it was almost the only way in which the pioneer learned what was going on in the East. But when discovery was made of the salt springs of the Kanawha, and the Holston, and Kentucky, and central New York, the West began to be freed from dependence on the coast. It was in part the effect of finding these salt springs that enabled settlement to cross the mountains.

From the time the mountains rose between the pioneer and the seaboard, a new order of Americanism arose. The West and the East began to get out of touch of each other. The settlements from the sea to the mountains kept connection with the rear and had a certain solidarity. But the over-mountain men grew more independent. The East took a narrow view of American advance, and nearly lost these men. Kentucky and Tennessee history bears abundant witness to the truth of this statement. The East began to try to hedge and limit westward expansion. Though Webster could declare that there were no Alleghenies in his politics, yet in politics in general they were a very solid factor.

The exploitation of the beasts took hunter and trader to the west, the exploitation of the grasses took the rancher west, and the exploitation of the virgin soil of the river valleys and prairies attracted the farmer. Good soils have been the most continuous attraction to the farmer's frontier. The land hunger of the Virginians drew them down the rivers into Carolina, in early colonial days; the search for soils took the Massachusetts men to Pennsylvania and to New York.
As the eastern lands were taken up migration flowed across them to the west. Daniel Boone, the great backwoodsman, who combined the occupations of hunter, trader, cattle-raiser, farmer, and surveyor --learning, probably from the traders, of the fertility of the lands of the upper Yadkin, where the traders were wont to rest as they took their way to the Indians--left his Pennsylvania home with his father, and passed down the Great Valley road to that stream. Learning from a trader of the game and rich pastures of Kentucky, he pioneered the way for the farmers to that region. Thence he passed to the frontier of Missouri, where his settlement was long a landmark on the frontier. Here again he helped to open the way for civilization, finding salt licks, and trails, and land. His son was among the earliest trappers in the passes of the Rocky Mountains, and his party are said to have been the first to camp on the present site of Denver. His grandson, Colonel A. J. Boone, of Colorado, was a power among the Indians of the Rocky Mountains, and was appointed an agent by the government. Kit Carson's mother was a Boone. Thus this family epitomizes the backwoodsman's advance across the continent.

The farmer's advance came in a distinct series of waves. In Peck's New Guide to the West, published in Boston in 1837, occurs this suggestive passage:

Generally, in all the western settlements, three classes, like the waves of the ocean, have rolled one after the other. First comes the pioneer, who depends for the subsistence of his family chiefly upon the natural growth of vegetation, called the "range," and the proceeds of hunting. His implements of agriculture are rude, chiefly of his own make, and his efforts directed mainly to a crop of corn and a "truck patch." The last is a rude garden for growing cabbage, beans, corn for roasting ears, cucumbers, and potatoes. A log cabin, and, occasionally, a stable and corn-crib, and a field of a dozen acres, the timber girdled or "deadened," and fenced, are enough for his occupancy. It is quite immaterial whether he ever becomes the owner of the soil. He is the occupant for the time being, pays no rent, and feels as independent as the "lord of the manor." With a horse, cow, and one or two breeders of swine, he strikes into the woods with his family, and becomes the founder of a new county, or perhaps state. He builds his cabin, gathers around him a few other families of similar tastes and habits, and occupies till the range is somewhat subdued, and hunting a little precarious, or, which is more frequently the case, till the neighbors crowd around, roads, bridges, and fields annoy him, and he lacks elbow room. The preemption law enables him to dispose of his cabin and cornfield to the next class of emigrants; and, to employ his own figures, he "breaks for the high timber," "clears out for the New Purchase," or migrates to Arkansas or Texas, to work the same process over.

The next class of emigrants purchase the lands, add field to field, clear out the roads, throw rough bridges over the streams, put up hewn log houses with glass windows and brick or stone chimneys, occasionally plant orchards, build mills, schoolhouses, courthouses, etc., and exhibit the picture and forms of plain, frugal, civilized life.

Another wave rolls on The men of capital and enterprise come. The settler is ready to sell out and take the advantage of the rise in property, push farther into the interior and become, himself, a man of capital, and enterprise in turn. The small village rises to a spacious town or city; substantial edifices of brick, extensive fields, orchards, gardens, colleges, and churches are seen. Broadcloths, silks, leghorns, crapes, and all the refinements, luxuries, elegancies, frivolities, and fashions are in vogue Thus wave after wave is rolling westward; the real Eldorado is still farther on.

A portion of the two first classes remain stationary amidst the general movement, improve their habits and condition, and rise in the scale of society. The writer has traveled much amongst the first class, the real pioneers. He has lived many years in connection with the second grade; and now the third wave is sweeping over large districts of Indiana, Illinois, and Missouri. Migration has become almost a habit in the West. Hundreds of men can be found, not over 50 years of age, who have settled for the fourth, fifth, or sixth time on a new spot. To sell out and remove only a few hundred miles makes up a portion of the variety of backwoods life and manners.

Omitting those of the pioneer farmers who move from the love of adventure, the advance of the more steady farmer is easy to understand. Obviously the immigrant was attracted by the cheap lands of the frontier, and even the native farmer felt their influence strongly. Year by year the farmers who lived on soil whose returns were diminished by un-rotated crops were offered the virgin soil of the frontier at nominal prices. Their growing families demanded more lands, and these were dear. The competition of the unexhausted, cheap, and easily tilled prairie lands compelled the farmer either to go west and continue the exhaustion of the soil on a new frontier, or to adopt intensive culture. Thus the census of 1890 shows, in the Northwest, many counties in which there is an absolute or a relative decrease of population. These States have been sending farmers to advance the frontier on the plains, and have themselves begun to turn to intensive farming and to manufacture. A decade before this, Ohio had shown the same transition stage. Thus the demand for land and the love of wilderness freedom drew the frontier ever onward.

Having now roughly outlined the various kinds of frontiers, and their modes of advance, chiefly from the point of view of the frontier itself, we may next inquire what were the influences on the East and on the Old World. A rapid enumeration of some of the more noteworthy effects is all that I have time for. First, we note that the frontier promoted the formation of a composite nationality for the American preponderantly English, but the later tides of continental immigration flowed across the free lands. This was the case from the early colonial days. The Scotch-Irish and the Palatine Germans, or "Pennsylvania Dutch," furnished the dominant eleme nt in the stock of the colonial frontier. With these peoples were also the freed indented servants, or redemptioners, who at the expiration of their time of service passed to the frontier. Governor Spotswood of Virginia writes in 1717, "The inhabitants of our frontiers are composed generally of such as have been transported hither as of their time, settle themselves where land is to be taken and that will produce the necessarys of life with little labour." Very generally these redemptioners were of non-English stock. In the crucible of the frontier the immigrants were Americanized, liberated, and fused into a mixed race, English in neither nationality nor characteristics. The process has gone on from the early days to our own. Burke and other writers in the middle of the eighteenth century believed that Pennsylvania was "threatened with the danger of being wholly foreign in language, manners and perhaps even inclinations." The German and Scotch-Irish elements in the frontier of the South were only less great. In the middle of the present century the German element in Wisconsin was already so considerable that leading publicists looked to the creation of a German state out of the commonwealth by concentrating their colonization. Such examples teach us to beware of misinterpreting the fact that there is a common English speech in America into a belief that the stock is also English.

In another way the advance of the frontier decreased our dependence on England. The coast, particularly of the South, lacked diversified industries, and was dependent on England for the bulk of its supplies. In the South there was even a dependence on the Northern colonies for articles of food. Governor Glenn, of South Carolina, writes in the middle of the eighteenth century: "Our trade with New York and Philadelphia was of this sort, draining us of all the little money and bills we could gather from other places for their bread, flour, beer, hams, bacon, and other things of their produce, all which, except beer, our new townships begin to supply us with, which are settled with very industrious and thriving Germans. This no doubt diminishes the number of shipping and the appearance of our trade, but it is far from being a detriment to us." Before long the frontier created a demand for merchants. As it retreated from the coast it became less and less possible for England to bring her supplies directly to the consumer's wharfs, and carry away staple crops, and staple crops began to give way to diversified agriculture for a time. The effect of this phase of the frontier action upon the northern section is perceived when we realize how the advance of the frontier aroused seaboard cities like Boston, New York, and Baltimore to engage in rivalry for what Washington called "the extensive and valuable trade of a rising empire.

The legislation which most developed the powers of the national government, and played the largest part in its activity, was conditioned on the frontier. Writers have discussed the subjects of tariff, land, and internal improvement, as subsidiary to the slavery question. But when American history comes to be rightly viewed it will be seen that the slavery question is an incident. In the period from the end of the first half of the present century to the close of the Civil War slavery rose to primary, but far from exclusive, importance. But this does not justify Dr. von Holst (to take an example) in treating our constitutional history in its formative period down to 1828 in a single volume, giving six volumes chiefly to the history of slavery from 1828 to 1861, under the title "Constitutional History of the United States." The growth of nationalism and the evolution of

American political institutions were dependent on the advance of the frontier. Even so recent a writer as Rhodes, in his "History of the United States since the Compromise of 1850," has treated the legislation called out by the western advance as incidental to the slavery struggle.

This is a wrong perspective. The pioneer needed the goods of the coast, and so the grand series of internal improvement and railroad legislation began, with potent nationalizing effects. Over internal improvements occurred great debates, in which grave constitutional questions were discussed. Sectional groupings appear in the votes, profoundly significant for the historian. Loose construction in-creased as the nation marched westward. But the West was not content with bringing the farm to the factory. Under the lead of Clay--"Harry of the West"--protective tariffs were passed, with the cry of bringing the factory to the farm. The disposition of the public lands was a third important subject of national legislation influenced by the frontier.

The public domain has been a force of profound importance in the nationalization and development of the government. The effects of the struggle of the landed and the landless States, and of the Ordinance of 1787, need no discussion. Administratively the frontier called out some of the highest and most vitalizing activities of the general government. The purchase of Louisiana was perhaps the constitutional turning point in the history of the Republic, inasmuch as it afforded both a new area for national legislation and the occasion of the downfall of the policy of strict construction. But the purchase of Louisiana was called out by frontier needs and demands.

As frontier States accrued to the Union the national power grew. In a speech on the dedication of the Calhoun monument Mr. Lamar explained: "In 1789 the States were the creators of the Federal Government; in 1861 the Federal Government was the creator of a large majority of the States."

When we consider the public domain from the point of view of the sale and disposal of the public lands we are again brought face to face with the frontier. The policy of the United States in dealing with its lands is in sharp contrast with the European system of scientific administration. Efforts to make this domain a source of revenue, and to withhold it from emigrants in order that settlement might be compact, were in vain. The jealousy and the fears of the East were powerless in the face of the demands of the frontiersmen. John Quincy Adams was obliged to confess: "My own system of administration, which was to make the national domain the inexhaustible fund for progressive and unceasing internal improvement, has failed." The reason is obvious: a system of administration was not what the West demanded: it wanted land. Adams states the situation as follows: "The slaveholders of the South have bought the cooperation of the western country by the bribe of the western lands, abandoning to the new Western States their own proportion of the public property and aiding them in the design of grasping all the lands into their own hands. Thomas H. Benton was the author of this system, which he brought forward as a substitute for the-American system of Mr. Clay, and to supplant him as the leading statesman of the West. Mr. Clay, by his tariff compromise with Mr. Calhoun, abandoned his own American system. At the same time he brought forward a plan for distributing among all the States of the Union the proceeds of the sales of the public lands. His bill for that purpose passed both Houses of Congress, but was vetoed by President Jackson, who, in his annual message of December, 1832, formally recommended that all public lands should be gratuitously given away to individual adventurers and to the States in which the lands are situated."

"No subject," said Henry Clay, "which has presented itself to the present, or perhaps any preceding Congress, is of greater magnitude than that of the public lands." When we consider the far-reaching effects of the government's land policy upon political, economic, and social aspects of American life, we are disposed to agree with him. But this legislation was framed under frontier influences, and under the lead of Western statesmen like Benton and Jackson. Said

Senator Scott of Indiana in 1841: "I consider the preemption law merely declaratory of the custom or common law of the settlers."

It is safe to say that the legislation with regard to land, tariff, and internal improvements--the American system of the nationalizing Whig party--was conditioned on frontier ideas and needs. But it was not merely in legislative action that the frontier worked against the sectionalism of the coast. The economic and social characteristics of the frontier worked against sectionalism. The men of the frontier had closer resemblances to the Middle region than to either of the other sections. Pennsylvania had been the seed-plot of frontier emigration, and, although she passed on her settlers along the Great Valley into the west of Virginia and the Carolinas, yet the industrial society of these Southern frontiersmen was always more like that of the Middle region than like that of the tidewater portion of the South, which later came to spread its industrial type throughout the South.

The Middle region, entered by New York harbor, was an open door to all Europe, The tidewater part of the South represented typical Englishmen, modified by a warm climate and servile labor, and living in baronial fashion on great plantations; New England stood for a special English movement--Puritanism. The Middle region was less English than the other sections. It had a wide mixture of nationalities, a varied society, the mixed town and county system of local government, a varied economic life, many religious sects. In short, it was a region mediating between New England and the South, and the East and the West. It represented that composite nationality which the contemporary United States exhibits, that juxtaposition of non-English groups, occupying a valley or a little settlement, and presenting reflections of the map of Europe in their variety. It was democratic and non-sectional, if not national; "easy, tolerant, and contented"; rooted strongly in material prosperity. It was typical of the modern United States. It was least sectional, not only because it lay between North and South, but also because with no barriers to shut out its frontiers from its settled region, and with a system of connecting waterways, the Middle region mediated between East and West as well as between North and South. Thus it became the typically American region. Even the New Englander, who was shut out from the frontier by the Middle region, tarrying in New York or Pennsylvania on his westward march, lost the acuteness of his sectionalism on the way.

The spread of cotton culture into the interior of the South finally broke down the contrast between the "tidewater" region and the rest of the State, and based Southern interests on slavery. Before this process revealed its results the western portion of the South, which was akin to Pennsylvania in stock, society, and industry, showed tendencies to fall away from the faith of the fathers into internal improvement legislation and nationalism. In the Virginia convention of 1829-30, called to revise the constitution, Mr. Leigh, of Chesterfield, one of the tidewater counties, declared:

One of the main causes of discontent which led to this convention, that which had the strongest influence in overcoming our veneration for the work of our fathers, which taught us to contemn the sentiments of Henry and Mason and Pendleton, which weaned us from our reverence for the constituted authorities of the State, was an overweening passion for internal improvement. I say this with perfect knowledge, for it has been avowed to me by gentlemen from the West over and over again. And let me tell the gentleman from Albemarle (Mr. Gordon) that it has been another principal object of those who set this ball of revolution in motion, to overturn the doctrine of State rights, of which Virginia has been the very pillar, and to remove the barrier she has interposed to the interference of the Federal Government in that same work of internal improvement, by so reorganizing the legislature that Virginia, too, may be hitched to the Federal car.

It was this nationalizing tendency of the West that transformed the democracy of Jefferson into the national republicanism of Monroe and the democracy of Andrew Jackson. The West of the War of 1812, the West of Clay, and Benton and Harrison, and Andrew Jackson, shut off by the Middle States and the mountains from the coast sections, had a solidarity of its own with national tendencies. On the tide of the Father of Waters, North and South met and mingled into a nation. Interstate migration went steadily on—a process of cross-fertilization of ideas and institutions. The fierce struggle of the sections over slavery on the western frontier does not diminish the truth of this statement; it proves the truth of it. Slavery was a sectional trait that would not down, but in the West it could not remain sectional. It was the greatest of frontiersmen who declared: "I believe this Government can not endure permanently half slave and half free. It will become all of one thing or all of the other." Nothing works for nationalism like intercourse within the nation. Mobility of population is death to localism, and the western frontier worked irresistibly in unsettling population. The effect reached back from the frontier and affected profoundly the Atlantic coast and even the Old World.

But the most important effect of the frontier has been in the promotion of democracy here and in Europe. As has been indicated the frontier is productive of individualism. Complex society is precipitated by the wilderness into a kind of primitive organization, based on the family. The tendency is anti-social. It produces antipathy to control, and particularly to any direct control. The tax-gatherer is viewed as a representative of oppression. Professor Osgood, in an able article, has pointed out that the frontier-conditions prevalent in the colonies are important factors in the explanation of the American Revolution, where individual liberty was sometimes confused with absence of all effective government. The same conditions aid in explaining the difficulty of instituting a strong government in the period of the confederacy. The frontier individualism has from the beginning promoted democracy.

The frontier States that came into the Union in the first quarter of a century of its existence came in with democratic suffrage provisions, and had reactive effects of the highest importance upon the older States whose peoples were being attracted there. An extension of the franchise became essential. It was western New York that forced an extension of suffrage in the constitutional convention of that State in 1821, and it was western Virginia that compelled the tidewater region to put a more liberal suffrage provision in the constitution framed in 1830, and to give to the frontier region a more nearly proportionate representation with the tidewater aristocracy.
The rise of democracy as an effective force in the nation came in with western preponderance under Jackson and William Henry Harrison, and it meant the triumph of the frontier--with all of its good and with all of its evil elements. An interesting illustration of the tone of frontier democracy in 1830 comes from the same debates in the Virginia convention already referred to. A representative from western Virginia declared:

But, sir, it is not the increase of population in the West which this gentleman ought to fear. It is the energy which the mountain breeze and western habits impart to those emigrants. They are regenerated, politically I mean, sir. They soon become working politicians; and the difference, sir, between a talking and a working politician is immense. The Old Dominion has long been celebrated for producing great orators; the ablest metaphysicians in policy; men that can split hairs in all abstruse questions of political economy. But at home, or when they return from Congress, they have Negroes to fan them asleep. But a Pennsylvania, a New York, an Ohio, or a western Virginia statesman, though far inferior in logic, metaphysics, and rhetoric to an old Virginia statesman, has this advantage, that when he returns home he takes off his coat and takes hold of the plow. This gives him bone and muscle, sir, and preserves his republican principles pure and uncontaminated.

So long as free land exists, the opportunity for a competency exists, and economic power secures political power. But the democracy born of free land, strong in selfishness and individualism, intolerant of administrative experience and education, and pressing individual liberty beyond its proper bounds, has its dangers as well as its benefits. Individualism in America has allowed a laxity in regard to governmental affairs which has rendered possible the spoils system and all the manifest evils that follow from the lack of a highly developed civic spirit. In this connection may be noted also the influence of frontier conditions in permitting lax business honor, inflated paper currency and wildcat banking. The colonial and revolutionary frontier was the region whence emanated many of the worst forms of an evil currency. The West in the War of 1812 repeated the phenomenon on the frontier of that day, while the speculation and wildcat banking of the period of the crisis of 1837 occurred on the new frontier belt of the next tier of States. Thus each one of the periods of lax financial integrity coincides with periods when a new set of frontier communities had arisen, and coincides in area with these successive frontiers, for the most part. The recent Populist agitation is a case in point. Many a State that now declines any connection with the tenets of the Populists, itself adhered to such ideas in an earlier stage of the development of the State. A primitive society can hardly be expected to show the intelligent appreciation of the complexity of business interests in a developed society. The continual recurrence of these areas of paper-money agitation is another evidence that the frontier can be isolated and studied as a factor in American history of the highest importance. The East has always feared the result of an unregulated advance of the frontier, and has tried to check and guide it. The English authorities would have checked settlement at the headwaters of the Atlantic tributaries and allowed the "savages to enjoy their deserts in quiet lest the peltry trade should decrease." This called out Burke's splendid protest:

"If you stopped your grants, what would be the consequence? The people would occupy without grants. They have already so occupied in many places. You can not station garrisons in every part of these deserts. If you drive the people from one place, they will carry on their annual tillage and remove with their flocks and herds to another. Many of the people in the back settlements are already little attached to particular situations. Already they have topped the Appalachian Mountains. From thence they behold before them an immense plain, one vast, rich level meadow; a square of;five hundred miles. Over this they would wander without a possibility of restraint; they would change their manners with their habits of life; would soon forget a government by which they were disowned; would become hordes of English Tartars; and, pouring down upon your unfortified frontiers a fierce and irresistible cavalry, become masters of your governors and your counselors, your collectors and comptrollers, and of all the slaves that adhered to them. Such would, and in no long time must, be the effect of attempting to forbid as a crime and to suppress as an evil the command and blessing of Providence, "Increase and multiply." Such would be the happy result of an endeavor to keep as a lair of wild beasts that earth which God, by an express charter, has given to the children of men."

But the English Government was not alone in its desire to limit the advance of the frontier and guide its destinies. Tidewater Virginia and South Carolina gerrymandered those colonies to insure the dominance of the coast in their legislatures. Washington desired to settle a State at a time in the Northwest; Jefferson would reserve from settlement the territory of his Louisiana Purchase north of the thirty-second parallel, in order to offer it to the Indians in exchange for their settlements east of the Mississippi. "When we shall be full on this side," he writes, "we may lay off a range of States on the western bank from the head to the mouth, and so range after range, advancing compactly as we multiply." Madison went so far as to argue to the French minister that the United States had no interest in seeing population extend itself on the right bank of the Mississippi, but should rather fear it. When the Oregon question was under debate, in 1824, Smyth, of Virginia, would draw an unchangeable line for the limits of the United States at the outer limit of two tiers of States beyond the Mississippi, complaining that the seaboard States were being drained of the flower of their population by the bringing of too much land into market. Even Thomas Benton, the man of widest views of the destiny of the West, at this stage of his career declared that along the ridge of the Rocky Mountains "the western limits of the Republic should be drawn, and the statue of the fabled god Terminus should be raised upon its highest peak, never to be thrown down." But the attempts to limit the boundaries, to restrict land sales and settlement, and to deprive the West of its share of political power were all in vain. Steadily the frontier of settlement advanced and carried with it individualism, democracy, and nationalism, and powerfully affected the East and the Old World.

The most effective efforts of the East to regulate the frontier came through its educational and religious activity, exerted by interstate migration and by organized societies. Speaking in 1835, Dr. Lyman Beecher declared: "It is equally plain that the religious and political destiny of our nation is to be decided in the West," and he pointed out that the population of the West "is assembled from all the States of the Union and from all the nations of Europe, and is rushing in like the waters of the flood, demanding for its moral preservation the immediate and universal action of those institutions which discipline the mind and arm the conscience and the heart. And so various are the opinions and habits, and so recent and imperfect is the acquaintance, and so sparse are the settlements of the West, that no homogeneous public sentiment can be formed to legislate immediately into being the requisite institutions. And yet they are all needed immediately in their utmost perfection and power. A nation is being 'born in a day.' . . . But what will become of the West if her prosperity rushes up to such a majesty of power, while those great institutions linger which are necessary to form the mind and the conscience and the heart of that vast world? It must not be permitted.... Let no man at the East quiet himself and dream of liberty, whatever may become of the West.... Her destiny is our destiny."

With the appeal to the conscience of New England, he adds appeals to her fears lest other religious sects anticipate her own. The New England preacher and school-teacher left their mark on the West. The dread of Western emancipation from New England's political and economic control was paralleled by her fears lest the West cut loose from her religion. Commenting in 1850 on reports that settlement was rapidly extending northward in Wisconsin, the editor of the Home Missionary writes: "We scarcely know whether to rejoice or mourn over this extension of our settlements. While we sympathize in whatever tends to increase the physical resources and prosperity of our country, we can not forget that with all these dispersions into remote and still remoter corners of the land the supply of the means of grace is becoming relatively less and less." Acting in accordance with such ideas, home missions were established and Western colleges were erected. As seaboard cities like Philadelphia, New York, and Baltimore strove for the mastery of Western trade, so the various denominations strove for the possession of the West. Thus an intellectual stream from New England sources fertilized the West. Other sections sent their missionaries; but the real struggle was between sects. The contest for power and the expansive tendency furnished to the various sects by the existence of a moving frontier must have had important results on the character of religious organization in the United States. The multiplication of rival churches in the little frontier towns had deep and lasting social effects. The religious aspects of the frontier make a chapter in our history which needs study.

From the conditions of frontier life came intellectual traits of profound importance. The works of travelers along each frontier from colonial days onward describe certain common traits, and these traits have, while softening down, still persisted as survival in the place of their origin, even when a higher social organization succeeded. The result is that to the frontier the American intellect owes its striking characteristics. That coarseness and strength combined with acuteness and inquisitiveness; that practical, inventive turn of mind, quick to find expedients; that masterful grasp of material things, lacking in the artistic but powerful to effect great ends; that restless, nervous energy; that dominant individualism, working for good and for evil, and withal that buoyancy and exuberance which comes with freedom--these are traits of the frontier, or traits called out elsewhere because of the existence of the frontier. Since the days when the fleet of Columbus sailed into the waters of the New World, America has been another name for opportunity, and the people of the United States have taken their tone from the incessant expansion which has not only been open but has even been forced upon them. He would be a rash prophet who should assert that the expansive character of American life has now entirely ceased. Movement has been its dominant fact, and, unless this training has no effect upon a people, the American energy will continually demand a wider field for its exercise. But never again will such gifts of free land offer themselves. For a moment, at the frontier, the bonds of custom are broken and unrestraint is triumphant. There is not tabula rasa. The stubborn American environment is there with its imperious summons to accept its conditions; the inherited ways of doing things are also there; and yet, in spite of environment, and in spite of custom, each frontier did indeed furnish a new field of opportunity, a gate of escape from the bondage of the past; and freshness, and confidence, and scorn of older society, impatience of its restraints and its ideas, and indifference to its lessons, have accompanied the frontier. What the Mediterranean Sea was to the Greeks, breaking the bond of custom, offering new experiences, calling out new institutions and activities, that, and more, the ever retreating frontier has been to the United States directly, and to the nations of Europe more remotely. And now, four centuries from the discovery of America, at the end of a hundred years of life under the Constitution, the frontier has gone, and with its going has closed the first period of American history.

"….the frontier has gone, and with its going has closed the first period of American history."

About Clum & Company

This book is produced by Clum & Company Old-West Productions in association with Trafford Publishing. Formed in July 1, 2002 Clum & Company is registered in the city of Moreno Valley, California.

The mission of Clum & Company is:

1. Help to promote and preserve the "Old-West" west heritage of the United States.

2. Promote gun safety through education by means of presentations, demonstrations and printed materials.

3. Raise funds to help those less fortunate with a focus on children. Funds may be raised through skit performances or sales of promotional merchandise.

The two main functions of the company are:

1. Provide skits of an old-west nature for entertainment and to promote the company's mission. Clum & Company is available for parties, corporate picnics, entertainment at municipal functions, parades, store openings, and any other functions where "period attired" actors are needed.

2. The production of historical-oriented printed material that includes this book and magazine articles.

Clum & Company Old-West Productions
PO Box 466
Moreno Valley, California 92556

clumandcompany@aol.com

October, 1881 (plus 121 years)

Gun-Safety Message

Despite living during a very violent time, Wyatt Earp was never shot or wounded. However, history records (January 12, 1876) that even Wyatt Earp came close to shooting himself with his own gun in a moment when safety took a back seat. In keeping with our mission of promoting gun safety, please remember the following gun-safety rules:

For Adults:

Always assume that a gun is loaded and ready to fire.
- Whenever handling a firearm, personally check it to make sure it is unloaded.
- Do not handle a firearm that you are not familiar with. Ask a knowledgeable person to instruct you on the correct and safe use of the weapon.
- When handing a person a firearm, hand it to them with the action open so they can see that it is unloaded and safe.
- Even if a firearm leaves your personal control unloaded, it could come back to you loaded. Check a firearm every time you handle it. No exceptions.

Never point a firearm at something you do not intend to destroy.
- Always keep the muzzle pointed in a safe direction so if fired, it will not cause injury.
- Never point a gun at yourself.
- Always be aware of the location of shooting companions.

Never place your finger on the trigger until you are ready to shoot.
- Spot your target, make the conscious decision to fire, align the target, then place your finger on the trigger.

Be sure of your target and it's surroundings.
- Never shoot at an object that you have not positively identified.
- Never shoot when your vision is compromised.
- Know where the projectile will go in case you miss.

Additionally:
- Be sure to shoot only where it is safe and legal.
- Never mix alcohol or drugs with firearms.
- Store and transport firearms and ammunition safely and in accordance with local/state laws.

Gun safety for children:

Whenever Clum & Company performs; we always start with the following gun safety message for children:

If you encounter a firearm, assume that it is real, not a toy. Then, do the following:

- **Stop!**
- **Don't touch!**
- **Get away!**
- **Go tell an adult!**

Bibliography

Arizona Citizen, The November 29, 1829 (newspaper from author's collection)

Boston Daily Advertiser, The December 30, 1871 (newspaper from author's collection)

Boze Bell, Bob *The Illustrated Life and Times Of Wyatt Earp* 1995

Boze Bell, Bob *Bad Men, Outlaws & Gunfighters Of The Old West* 1999

Chaffin, Earl *It All Happened In Tombstone* by John Clum Edited by Earl Chaffin 1929 Clum 1999 Chaffin

Chaffin. Earl *Wyatt Earp in Alaska* 1999

Chaffin, Earl *An Arizona Vendetta The Truth About Wyatt Earp* by Forrestine Cooper Hooker Edited By Earl Chaffin Hooker 1919 Chaffin 1998

Chaffin, Earl *Wyatt's Woman The Recollections of Josephine Marcus Earp* Edited By Earl Chaffin Earp 1938 Chaffin 1998

Chaput, Don *Dr. Goodfellow Physician To The Gunfighters, Scholar, and Bon Vivant* 1996

Clayton, Wallace & Traywick, Ben *The Tombstone Epitaph & John Clum* 1985

Erdos, Richard *Saloons Of The Old West* 1979

Flanagan, Mike *The Old West Day By Day* 1995

Olsen, Hazel *The Traveling Earps* 1994

O' Neal, Bill *Ghost Town of the American West* 1995

Severa, Joan *Dressed For The Photographer – Ordinary Americans and Fashion 1840-1900* 1995

Tefertiller, Casey *Wyatt Earp – The Man Behind The Legend* 1997

Traywick, Ben *Ghost Towns & Lost Treasure* 1994

Ward, Geoffrey C. *The West - An Illustrated History* 1996

Young, Roy B. *Cochise County Cowboy War – A Cast Of Characters* 1999

Young, Roy B. *Pete Spence "Audacious Artist In Crime"* 2000

ISBN 155395129-8

9 781553 951292